The Therapeutic Toolbox

103 Group Activities

and **T**REATMENT

IDEAS &

PRACTICAL

STRATEGIES

Judith A. Belmont, MS, LPC

PESI Publishing & Media
www.pesi.com/publishing

Copyright © 2006

PESI Publishing & Media
PESI, Inc.
3839 White Avenue
Eau Claire, Wisconsin 54703
www.pesi.com/publishing

Printed in the United States of America

ISBN: 978-0979021800

PUB011340

ACKNOWLEDGMENTS

This book was inspired by the clients and workshop participants throughout the years who have let me into their lives and given me the opportunity to learn so much. I am particularly indebted to one of my very first jobs, the "Why Not" program in Worcester, MA, as this program sparked me to pursue my passion in promoting "hands-on" mental wellness education. Later, The Center for Humanistic Change in Bath, PA, furthered my knowledge and expertise in this area. Both settings laid the foundation and offered the creative tools and mindset that have served as a base and inspiration for my work. Thanks to Michael Olson from PESI who has spurred my interest in writing this therapeutic guide. Special thanks above all to my husband, Don, and three wonderful sons, Justin, Brian, and Adam, who have been the best supports, teachers, and guides of all!

TABLE OF CONTENTS

INTRODUCTION

This book is chock full of therapeutic ideas to use with all types of groups and is a compilation of the many tips and strategies I have gleaned in over 30 years of counseling experience. These activities and T.I.P.S. can be used in therapy groups for adolescents and adults, as well as in workplace wellness seminars and other group settings. It has been my longstanding belief that a therapist often needs to be prepared with tools to assume the role of life skills educator and trainer. This book offers ideas on how to incorporate life skills training into your work with groups. The focus on life skills is crucial for helping clients develop "hands-on" tools to progress successfully through therapy. Life skills training is not often a part of formal conventional education, and this workbook tries to help people learn coping strategies sorely lacking in formal education. This workbook helps the mental health professional assist group members in taking a proactive approach to the therapeutic process. Through experiential activities, exercises, self-help worksheets, and educational handouts, the individual can experience change—not just talk about it. For even the most treatment resistant client, these T.I.P.S. for your therapeutic toolbox can be life altering. These active T.I.P.S., tools, and techniques are especially helpful for those with characterological issues, where traditional "talking" treatment alone often proves inadequate.

As Confucius said, "Teach me and I will forget, show me and I will remember, involve me and I will understand."

This book is designed to help those in the mental health field, including anyone promoting "mental fitness / mental wellness," whether it be in the outpatient or inpatient setting, private office, or business world.

Within the T.I.P.S. approach, Therapeutic Ideas and Practical Strategies are broken down further into working TIPs for each activity, handout, or strategy. The TIP acronym contained within the various handouts and activities stands for Theory, Implementation, and Processing.

Any material in this book may be copied for your individual or group use with your own clients. If, however, there is interest in using any of these T.I.P.S. in any type of publication, it is required that permission be granted by the publisher.

QUOTES ON FLEXIBLE THINKING

"The bend in the road is not the end of the road unless you refuse to take the turn."

—Unknown

* * *

"To the man who only has a hammer, everything he encounters begins to look like a nail."

—Abraham H. Maslow

* * *

"Nothing is softer or more flexible than water, yet nothing can resist it."

—Lao Tzu

* * *

"There are things known and there are things unknown, and in between are the doors of perception."

—Aldous Huxley

* * *

"All our knowledge has its origin in our perceptions."

—Leonardo Da Vinci

Flexible Thinking

T.I.P.s #1 & #2
"HANDS-ON" EXERCISES FOR FLEXIBLE THINKING

THEORY: These simple exercises are two of my favorites, and they go literally "hand in hand" to start a group thinking creatively. They are great warm-ups for a therapeutic group, workplace wellness workshop, or training seminar. In a group situation, this is a short but very powerful exercise that involves everyone. Although you can do this exercise with clients in individual treatment and make a very compelling case for the importance of flexible thinking, the group experience is ideal so that individuals can see firsthand that what is natural for us is not always natural for others. This focus of being flexible in slightly shifting one's perspective is demonstrated powerfully yet simply in these two exercises.

T.I.P. #1 Finger Exercise—Get a Grip!

T.I.P. #2 Arm Folding Activity

T.I.P. #1 IMPLEMENTATION: Ask participants to clasp their hands so that their fingers interlock. Ask them to note which thumb is on top. In a group situation, ask them to raise their hands if they had their left thumb on top like me (noting to them that they can unclasp their hands now to raise their hands!). Usually roughly half the group raises their hands, regardless of right- or left-handedness. How many had their right thumb on top? Note the percentage now raising their hands. Note that what feels natural for some is not natural for others. Relate that idea to the idea of our perceptions; for example, we think people should see things the same way we do, and through this hands-on exercise we realize this is not true! Now have the group shift their fingers in the opposite way (make sure they clasp all their fingers differently, not just the thumbs). Ask the group how this feels. You likely will get responses such as, "weird, strange, uncomfortable." Apply this hands-on exercise as a metaphor for the importance of how we often need to shift our thinking just so slightly—even though it might seem unnatural—in order to look at a situation in a different way. This can be a visual reminder of the importance of being flexible and changing one's perspective, and to realizing that some people may struggle with something that might come naturally to you! In short, this exercise helps people "get a grip!"

T.I.P. #2 IMPLEMENTATION: Following the exercise in T.I.P. #1, have participants perform a more "advanced version." In this exercise, have everyone fold their arms, noting which arm is on top. Ask for hands (urging them to let go first, of course) for those who had their right arm on top, etc. Bring to their attention that many people who began with their right thumb on top in T.I.P. #1 will have the opposite arm on top in this exercise. As in T.I.P. #1, the group likely will be roughly evenly split. Now have the group try it the other way. This usually gives way to giggles as some group members circle around a bit before finding their position. Most participants claim it feels "even weirder" than in T.I.P. #1, which gives you the opportunity to re-emphasize that what feels natural to some may be a stretch to others, and vice versa. Again, this provides a metaphor for the idea that people perceive things differently. We often assume inaccurately that others are innately more like us than they really are, which can be a frustrating misperception! (An interesting variation on this exercise is having the group fold their legs instead.)

PROCESSING: These are quick and easy hands-on examples of how some people might looks at things in a more rational, healthy way, and some of us need to adjust our perceptions slightly in a way that is uncomfortable to us while very natural for others. How easy it is to comprehend how interpersonal mis-understandings occur in light of considering the lesson from these hands-on activities! We also often assume that people process things the way we do; we tend to assume too much rather than open up our minds. Encourage members that when they are under stress or depressed, anxious, etc. they can remind themselves to slightly shift perspective. One can shift those fingers to nudge oneself out of the one-dimensional thinking that often makes people feel stuck!

T.I.P.s #3–5
EXERCISES TO OPEN YOUR MIND!

THEORY: The human brain has incredible potential, but all too often we do not tap this unlimited potential as we look at things in routine, fixed ways. The creative potential of our minds is there for the exploring. Being stuck in habitual old patterns of routine thinking is limiting, and these T.I.P.s offer inroads to develop creative thinking skills. These exercises can be used individually but often are more powerful within the group experience.

T.I.P. #3 Brainteaser: Do You Know Your Roman Numerals?

T.I.P. #4 Brainteaser with Numbers

T.I.P. #5 Brainteaser with a One-Track Mind

T.I.P. #3 IMPLEMENTATION: Using a flipchart or dry erase board, ask volunteers to come up and brainstorm alternative ways to write the concept "three degrees below zero." After some tries, I narrow this request by asking them to find a way to write "three degrees below zero" using only one number. I have yet to have someone give this response:

$$\frac{0}{\text{M.D.}}$$
Ph.D.
B.A.

T.I.P. #4 IMPLEMENTATION: Whether in an individual or group format, ask clients if they are familiar with roman numerals. Generally most people are. Put IX on a flipchart or dry erase board and ask what number this represents. Most will know the answer is 9. Subsequently, instruct them to use one line to transform what is written there from 9 to 6. Most people think of lines being straight, but no one said the line could not be wavy! Add a wavy line producing:

SIX

T.I.P. #5 IMPLEMENTATION: Hold up a piece of white paper and ask, "What color is this?" (Group participants answer "White.") "What color is this?" ("White.") Then again, "What color is this?" ("White.") Then ask, "First thing that comes to your mind . . . what do cows drink?" Invariably you will get "milk" as the first response and then the correct response, "water," a few seconds after that. Urge participants to use this exercise to acknowledge how much we get trapped in traditional ways of thinking and at times are outright wrong through thinking in habitual, automatic ways. Along the same lines, you can ask "Who is Casper?" ("A ghost.") "Who is Casper?" ("A ghost.") "Who is Casper?" ("A ghost.") Then say, "First thing that comes to your mind . . . what do you put in the toaster? Invariably you will get "toast" as the first response unless there is a pause before you hear the correct answer, "bread."

PROCESSING: These three exercises demonstrate the importance of flexible thinking. The point is clear that once we have a stubborn mindset, our first inclinations often are misguided. We need to step back from our habitual habits of perception, and re-evaluate some of our judgments, which are based mostly on routine past judgments. Refreshing our perspective can provide us with the ability to perceive things more accurately, without bias and preconceptions.

T.I.P. #6
VISUAL ACTIVITY: LOOKING AT THINGS IN A DIFFERENT WAY

THEORY: We all can agree that there are different ways of looking at the same thing. These examples of famous visual drawings highlight this idea. These optical illusions bring home the point that there is more than one way of perceiving things around us. Being stuck in one-dimensional thinking can indeed be limiting!

IMPLEMENTATION: (Before group, photocopy the images on the following page to pass around the group.) Ask group members to look at the images. What do they see? Most often they will see one picture first, and some need no help quickly seeing the other figure. Others, however, have a great deal of trouble seeing the two pictures within the same picture.

PROCESSING: Encourage the group to view this visual activity as a way to emphasize the importance of flexible thinking skills. At times we are so stuck on one way of looking at something that we at times find it difficult to shift perspective slightly to see another equally valid interpretation of a situation. Rigid, one-dimensional thinking will only serve to cause one to miss out on important information, causing one to lose sight of the "whole." This tends to render us at times ineffective and inflexible in our thinking.

18

T.I.P. #7
BRAINTEASER: EVEN THE MOST PUZZLING SITUATIONS HAVE ANSWERS!

THEORY: We restrict our potential by thinking in habitual ways. Clients who are depressed or anxious can be encouraged that by thinking in creative new ways, new insights can be achieved. This is a fun brainstorming exercise for a group situation, training, or teambuilding. It also gives one hope that, as the title in this exercise suggests, even the most puzzling situations have answers!

T.I.P. #7 Handout: Puzzling Situations Brainteasers

IMPLEMENTATION: Have group members break up into groups of twos or threes. Give participants three minutes to decipher the messages in the riddles found in the "Puzzling Situations Brainteasers" handout. Or, you can consider them as a whole group without pairing off, depending on if you want this to be a small group exercise or a whole group exercise. (Answers are seen at the bottom of this page.) This exercise encourages creative, "out of the box" thinking, which can be key in successfully dealing with psychological and relationship problems.

PROCESSING: Encourage individuals to see these "puzzles" as representations of their puzzling life situations. Ask participants how they felt and what this taught them about the importance of thinking in different ways. Encourage them to realize that thinking creatively and changing their perspectives often presents untapped potential. Creative and flexible thinking expands awareness to problem-solve in ways that can challenge and conquer even the most daunting dilemmas.

Answers: 1. Tea for two 2. Mayonnaise 3. Misunderstanding 4. Full back, halfback, quarterback 5. Once upon a time 6. Painless Operation 7. Are you lonesome without me? 8. Car in reverse gear 9. Mixed drinks

PUZZLING SITUATIONS BRAINTEASERS

1.

1T3456789

2.

MAY
AA

3.

Standing
UNDER

4.

BACK
BA
B

5.

11
TIME

6.

O-ER-T-I-O-

7.

Areyouloneso

8.

RcAaErG

9.

dknisr
krinds
rknisd

"GROUPIE" QUOTES

"The well-run group is not a battlefield of egos."

—Lao Tzu

* * *

"Individuals play the game, but teams win championships.

—Unknown

* * *

"Good communication is as stimulating as black coffee, and just as hard to sleep after."

—Anne Morrow Lindbergh

* * *

"Never doubt that a small group of thoughtful, committed citizens can change the world; indeed, it's the only thing that ever has."

—Margaret Mead

Group Beginnings

T.I.P.s #8–#10
ACTIVITIES FOR GROUP INTRODUCTIONS: THE NAME GAMES

THEORY: Introductions set a tone for the ongoing group process. First impressions often have long-lasting effects! Creative, fun ways to help members bond and disclose in a non-threatening manner tend to start a group off on the right foot. This creative method of introducing oneself to others encourages members to participate right off the bat.

T.I.P. #8 Name Association Activity

T.I.P. #9 Learning and Remembering Names

T.I.P. #10 Yet Another "Name Game" Activity

T.I.P. #8 IMPLEMENTATION: Begin the group session by explaining that you would like group members to **1.** introduce themselves with first name only, **2.** use the first letter of their first name to describe something about themselves, and **3.** use the first letter of their last name to name something they like. For example, in the case of someone with the initials G.I., a response could be, "My name is Gina, and I am Gracious, and I like Ice Cream." Once everyone has had a turn, use T.I.P. #9 to ensure that all names are remembered.

T.I.P. #9 IMPLEMENTATION: With so many names to remember, it is often difficult to keep names straight when embarking on a new group experience. This activity offers a very effective way to help group members remember names. Ask for a volunteer to try to go around and say as many names as possible, while encouraging group members to chime in to correct or help out. After the first volunteer, ask for another volunteer, repeating this exercise until all names are stated correctly at least a couple of times.

T.I.P. #10 IMPLEMENTATION: This is another variation of a "name game." Using a large, soft ball, such as a beach ball, start the "ball rolling" by saying your name and the first thing that comes to mind to describe something about yourself. By asking for the "first thing," participants are not likely to feel too put on the spot, as there is no expectation to have something prepared. Suggested topics participants can choose could be a like or dislike, thought, interest, occupation, or how they feel at the moment. Have all members take a turn at having the ball thrown to them. Once it goes back for a second round, say your name again and this time respond to something someone else had said. This 2nd version makes for an entertaining and interactive way to introduce oneself while listening to others.

PROCESSING: These three introduction activities set an interactive tone right from the start. You might brainstorm with participants on how to remember people's names for future group sessions—perhaps associating their names with something mentioned in T.I.P. #8. Talk about first impressions and discuss what they learned about one another from the adjective each participant chose. After using any of the three T.I.P.s, ask how the group felt about introducing themselves in these ways and what they learned about others.

T.I.P. #11
GROUP ACTIVITY: GETTING TO KNOW YOU

THEORY: Personal introductions are a way to start the group off on a positive note. This activity sets the stage for active participation and small group sharing right from the beginning. It also encourages the use of listening skills and gives participants an opportunity to glean important information about their fellow group members while getting a chance to express themselves.

IMPLEMENTATION: In the first session, do a self-introduction, and then request that all members pair up in twos or threes to introduce themselves to one another. Request that they find out the following: The person's first name, how they describe themselves, something about themselves that they think might be of interest to others, and what they hope to get out of the group experience. The partners might want to take notes in order to introduce these members to the group afterward. Give group members five to eight minutes (depending on if you pair into twos or threes), and then have the small groups take turns introducing one another to the whole group.

PROCESSING: This activity emphasizes active listening, learning, and sharing with one another. It gives everyone a chance to participate in the group experience. It has many advantages over the more traditional manner of self-introduction, as this activity is very interactive and requires listening and learning.

T.I.P. #12
ACTIVITY: TRUTHS & UNTRUTHS

THEORY: This is a fun and potentially intriguing activity for a newly formed group, and a way to get to know one another while getting a chance to play detective!

IMPLEMENTATION: In this activity, have all group members write down two things about themselves that are true and one or two "untruths." Items can include something that seems plausible or something outlandish—that is up to each individual. Then go around and have each person say the two truths and one or two untruths, and ask group members to guess which are true and which are not. After a minute or so of guessing, the "real" answers are shared. Have them explain their deductive reasoning. Make sure all participants get a turn.

PROCESSING: Ask group members what they found out about each person from the "true" statements and what they found about each person by the "untruths." This is a good activity for self-disclosure and for developing group cohesiveness.

> I have been skydiving,
> I've been to Alaska,
> and I am a lawyer.

T.I.P. #13
ICEBREAKER ACTIVITY: CATCH!

THEORY: This is a light-hearted, informal exercise in which members are given an opportunity to share about themselves with the group. This need not only be for introduction purposes. This activity also can be used in an ongoing group to give all members a chance to express.

IMPLEMENTATION: Using a beach ball or other large, soft ball, start the "ball rolling" by having members take turns throwing the ball to one another. Upon receiving the ball, each member makes a self-disclosure (such as something he/she did that week, something on his/her mind, etc.), and then throws the ball to someone else. After everyone gets a turn, the leader could have another topic for the next round, for instance, naming a favorite song and why; the next round could be another question such as, "What is the best (or worst) thing that happened to you this week?" Questions can be tailored to the type of group and what issues you would like addressed in the group.

PROCESSING: This informal activity encourages even the quietest member of the group to participate and can be a springboard for addressing issues relating to the leader's questions. The playfulness symbolized by the ball can underlie very serious disclosure in a relatively non-threatening manner.

T.I.P. #14
ACTIVITY: INITIALLY CREATED

THEORY: This short activity gives creative license to each individual. This light-hearted exercise might tap some creative juices he/she did not even know he/she possessed!

IMPLEMENTATION: Although this can be done in individual treatment, particularly for a low functioning individual who has little confidence in creativity, a group format is ideal. Supply all group members with paper and a writing utensil. Ask them to write their initials and then make a picture from those initials. Allow about five to ten minutes. Caution them that this can be a very simple picture. At first, you might be met by groans and resistance, but many people surprise themselves by developing some whimsical, creative pictures. Then have group members share with one another; this often leads to laughter and lightness!

PROCESSING: This teaches participants that they might have more creative reserve than they give themselves credit for, and encourages them to tap their creativity and flexibility. Remind them that keeping an open mind allows for creative self-expression.

T.I.P. #15
ACTIVITY: HUMAN SCAVENGER HUNT

THEORY: This activity is a fun, interactive way of either getting to know people in a new group or establishing more connection in an already established group. The object of this activity is to find what participants have in common with one another. In a very short period of time, participants get to interact with all of the group members and find one of the universal truths of groups—that they are not alone!

T.I.P. #15 Handout: Human Scavenger Hunt

IMPLEMENTATION: On the next page is the "Human Scavenger Hunt" handout containing items for group members. For the first couple of minutes, have members circle or fill in whatever items they choose to. Then instruct them to go around and find others with the same answers, having others initial answers that they have in common. If it is an already established group, you can make the questions more complex, perhaps pertaining to the themes of the group's needs.

PROCESSING: This activity is a great icebreaker and teambuilding activity, as well as a great way to connect with others more personally. This activity establishes a sense of group universality and camaraderie. Participants get to find out a lot of information about one another in a very short period of time. Expect a lot of laughter and smiles while participants do this exercise.

HUMAN SCAVENGER HUNT

INSTRUCTIONS: Fill in below any items that you wish to; then find others who have the same answers. Have them initial next to an item you have in common.

Find groups members who share your answers for the following answers:

1. Favorite color _____

2. Marital status _____

3. Children? If so, how many? Boys? Girls? _____

4. Furthest place to which you have traveled _____

5. Favorite type of exercise _____

6. Favorite movie _____

7. Favorite book _____

8. Favorite food _____

9. If you won the lottery, what's the first thing you would buy? ___

10. Car you drive _____

11. One word to describe yourself _____

12. Favorite type of nature scene _____

13. Favorite winter sport _____

14. Favorite fair weather sport _____

15. Favorite type of restaurant _____

16. Number of siblings _____

17. Favorite type of music _____

18. Favorite day of the week _____

19. What's the first thing you do when you get home? _____

20. What did you eat for breakfast this morning? _____

21. What color is the front door of your house? _____

22. Last big purchase _____

23. How many pets? What kind? _____

24. Favorite hobby _____

T.I.P. #16
ACTIVITY: THE CIRCLE GAME

THEORY: It is ideal to begin a group experience with everyone involved. It sets an interactive tone for the group, and this fun activity is a great way for people to connect personally with others in a short period of time. This activity promotes group cohesiveness while offering the opportunity for non-threatening self-disclosure.

IMPLEMENTATION: In this exercise there needs to be at least ten people in the group, and it can accommodate up to about 40 if you are conducting a skills training seminar or an in-service teambuilding training. Have group members count off by twos. Have all the number ones form a circle, and then face outward. Have all the number twos face any of the number ones. Ask the group a question from the sample questions below, or make up your own, specific to the nature of the group. The larger the group, the more limited the time should be for each question. After about two to three minutes, ask for everyone's attention and ask the outside circle to move one person to the right. Ask another question. Repeat this as much as time allows or approximately 15 minutes. This gives people a chance to meet as many people as possible. You might need a microphone when you go on to the next question, since it might be difficult to carry your voice over the talking.

The Circle Game Sample Questions

What would you be doing if you were not here?

What do you hope to learn today in this group?

What do you want to know about the other person? Ask one question.

Say one thing about yourself that you are happy about.

Say one thing about yourself that you need to work on.

Complete the sentence, "In the last year, I have learned . . ."

If you had a logo, what would it be?

Share something most people do not know about you.

Share something you are most proud of.

Name your favorite hobbies or interests.

Explain what you wish for the most.

If you were an animal, what would you be and why?

Name a favorite book or movie. Explain briefly.

Name one dream or wish you have.

Complete the sentence, "I would like to understand . . ."

PROCESSING: Be prepared for an animated experience as people often linger and have to be urged to move on. They often have not finished their conversations! This makes people eager to participate in the group experience, and already there is a sense of bonding, especially if this activity is used in the first session. A variation of this would be for a group closing, where you also want to give people an opportunity to share and touch base with one another.

T.I.P. #17
ACTIVITY: COLORFUL GROUP SURVEY

THEORY: This "group survey" is one of my favorite ways to get everyone to participate and gain a lot of information, all without saying a word! This is a great exercise for all types of therapeutic groups as well as "workplace wellness" groups. All members give input without "putting themselves on the line." This is also a very colorful, visual, and fun way to find out where the group is at any given time.

IMPLEMENTATION: Tape some pieces of newsprint on the wall and have questions written on each. The topic and theme of the therapeutic group or workshop will determine the type of questions that you will use (examples are on the following page). Have available self-adhesive colored dots from an office supply store, and you can decide if you want to have men take one color and women another to differentiate between how the two groups respond, or think of other ways to distinguish two or more types of subgroups, such as by age. Have the questions already up on newsprint, and ask people when they first come in to put a dot next to each item that they feel describes how they think or feel, with no more than one dot for each piece of newsprint. I use this activity in stress management workshops in particular to poll the habits of thinking, self-care, exercise, and so forth. This also has worked well in groups focusing on interpersonal communication and dealing with difficult people. By the time the group session begins, members will already have gleaned a lot of information about one another. Summarize the findings and brainstorm what they take from this "informal poll."

PROCESSING: Be prepared to analyze and summarize the results for the whole group. To have a more interactive process, however, have participants assist you in drawing conclusions based on the survey results. Count the dots together and make observations about how people handle stress, relationships, and so on, based on survey findings. Through your choice of questions, you can introduce the importance of concepts you wish to explore in a particular group. This is certainly more colorful and creative than a formal agenda!

SAMPLE GROUP SURVEY QUESTIONS

- Most of my concerns are . . .

Other people's effects on me	Job
Coworkers	Health
Children	Finances
Myself	Other people's problems

- Hours of TV watched per week . . .

18 or more	10
15	6
12	less than 4

- When I am angry, I tend to . . .

Keep it in	Eat too much
Think about it rationally	Explode
Tell someone	Feel tense
Snap at others	

- Hours of exercise per week . . .

  0–1   2–3   4–5   6–7   8–9

- Under stress, I tend to . . .

  Look on the bright side of things
  Look at the down side of things

- In stressful times, I . . .

Get moody	Blow up
Feel composed	Withdraw
Sleep too much	Sleep too little

- When I am upset, I tend to . . .

Share it with someone	Keep it in
Eat	Exercise
Have physical symptoms	Get depressed

- I often take things seriously
- I often see the humor in things

36

Judith A. Belmont, M.S. (2006) • *The Therapeutic Toolbox: 103 Group Activities and T.I.P.S.* • www.worksiteinsights.com • All rights reserved.

- I feel relaxed most of the time
- I feel stressed most of the time
- There is so much to do I am constantly playing catch up

- The main things that cause me trouble are . . .

    Within my control
    Out of my control

- I feel involved in community activities
- I feel uninvolved

GROUP DISCOVERY QUOTES

"A dream you dream alone is only a dream. A dream you dream together is reality."

—John Lennon

* * *

"Alone we can do so little; together we can do so much."

—Helen Keller

* * *

"We must all hang together or most assuredly we will all hang separately."

—Benjamin Franklin

* * *

"We Learn . . .
10% of what we read
20% of what we hear
30% of what we see
50% of what we see and hear
70% of what we discuss
80% of what we experience
95% of what we teach others."

—William Glasser

Group Discovery

T.I.P.s #18–#21
SELF-DISCOVERY AND GROUP SHARING ACTIVITIES

THEORY: Sometimes the path to self-discovery and group sharing requires few words. This exercise entails whole group participation—everyone is involved and everyone gets a chance to express themselves and see how others view them. This can be a fun activity for non-threatening individual revelation.

T.I.P. #18 Activity: My Logo

T.I.P. #19 Activity: My "Dream" Logo

T.I.P. #20 Activity: I'll Show You What I Think!

T.I.P. #21 Activity: Group Logo

T.I.P. #18 IMPLEMENTATION: Supply group members with a sheet of paper and colored pencils or markers. Ask them to think for a few minutes of a Logo that symbolizes how they see themselves and draw a logo using that image. After all have finished, take turns giving everyone a chance to share his/her logo. What is the message or theme portrayed?

T.I.P. #19 IMPLEMENTATION: With a sheet of paper and colored pencils or markers, ask group participants to make their "dream" logo—how they would represent themselves if all their dreams came true and they accomplished all they dreamed of in their lives. You can contrast that with the logo they made from T.I.P. #18. As in the previous T.I.P., have the members go around and share their new logos and have them contrast their "dream" logo from their actual one. Have them brainstorm the differences between them and what steps they can take now to make their "dream" logo their actual logo.

T.I.P. #20 IMPLEMENTATION: A potentially comical, interesting, and fun variation is to have group members design logos for one another. This works best for a small group where members already know one another. Instruct them the logos cannot be critical or judgmental. Try this with a family and you are bound to get them on the "lighter side" of one another—as long as you caution that the logo cannot be a disparaging one. It can be all in good clean fun!

T.I.P. #21 IMPLEMENTATION: Another teambuilding activity is to create a team logo; have the group as a whole brainstorm and make one all together on the same newsprint. This is for a group who has been with one another for a while so that group themes can be easily conceptualized.

PROCESSING: These four T.I.P. variations allow for creativity in viewing oneself and others. The fact that minimal verbal skills are required can be a bonus for the very shy and quiet group member. These activities help people crystallize what is essential to their personas both from within and without. Logo activities also provide opportunity for supportive group feedback. T.I.P.s #20 and #21 are especially great for team spirit and group cohesiveness. These are also great activities with families for developing more cohesiveness. Ingrained negative patterns become "unstuck" during these creative exercises. In addition, these afford opportunity to reinforce healthy boundaries in enmeshed family systems, as each distinct individual has his/her own message apart from the group message. All four activities are fun, creative outlets for self-expression and offer opportunity to share and bond with others.

T.I.P. #22
ACTIVITY:
MY, HAVE YOU CHANGED!

THEORY: This is a fun group exercise to teach the importance of being observant in dealing with change. It teaches the concept of mindfulness, as participants are encouraged to be present-focused and aware. How often we find ourselves so wrapped up in our own thoughts and feelings that we do not keenly observe the world around us!

IMPLEMENTATION: Ask group members to stand and break into pairs. Have them look carefully at one another, observing as much as they can about the other person's dress, hairstyle, etc. Then have them face apart with their backs to one another. Have the tallest person of each pair alter two things about his/her appearance. When they then turn around, the partner has 30 to 45 seconds to figure out what has changed. They have no more then 10 guesses. Then have them switch roles and repeat. Whichever members got both right get to remain in the activity, and the others sit out. Those that remain standing will need to pair up again with another partner do so. If there is an odd number, you as facilitator step in to be the one in a pair who alters your appearance.

PROCESSING: This exercise emphasizes the importance of being more "mindful." This can be a great opportunity to explain and demonstrate the importance of mindfulness, where one learns to be a keen observer of the world.

QUOTES ON COMMUNICATION

"The most important thing in communication is to hear what isn't being said."

—Peter F. Drucker

* * *

"There is nothing so annoying as to have two people talking when you're busy interrupting."

—Mark Twain

* * *

"Why do we hear such everlasting negative talk! People all imagine they'll be giving something away if they recognize the least bit of merit."

—Johann Wolfgang von Goethe

* * *

"Communication—the human connection—is the key to personal and career success."

—Paul J. Meyer

* * *

"If you want to make peace, you don't talk to your friends. You talk to your enemies."

—Mother Teresa of Calcutta

* * *

We have two ears and one mouth so that we can listen twice as much as we speak."

—Epictetus

Communication 101

T.I.P.s #23–#26
ROLE-PLAY SCENES: LEARNING THE DIFFERENCES BETWEEN ASSERTIVE, AGGRESSIVE, AND NON-ASSERTIVE COMMUNICATION

THEORY: We all know the difference between the three major types of communication—assertive, aggressive, and non-assertive. It's just plain obvious. Right? WRONG! Even though the differences seem obvious to most on the surface, once this role-play is enacted, there are numerous opinions as to which type of communication was being portrayed each time. It is no wonder, therefore, that disagreements, arguments, and conflict are much too common in close interpersonal relationships. It's not as easy as it seems to discern what is and is not appropriate behavior. This exercise does a great job of helping people become more observant and insightful about their own communication style and that of others.

T.I.P. #23 Aggressive Role-Play Scenario: Dinner Meeting Scene

T.I.P. #24 Non-Assertive Role-Play Scenario: Dinner Meeting Scene

T.I.P. #25 Assertive Role-Play Scenario: Dinner Meeting Scene

T.I.P. #26 Handout: Assertive, Aggressive, and Non-Assertive Behavior

IMPLEMENTATION: Begin by introducing the concept that the importance of communication cannot be overstated. Jobs, marriages, and relationships are made or broken due to communication skills. Despite the importance of communication skills, however, we often are not taught this fundamental lesson in schools, and miscommunication is all too common. In both therapeutic groups and professional or workplace seminars, I begin by asking people if they know these three types of communication. Usually nearly everyone raises their hands. I caution them that although many of us think we know the differences, in everyday life we often have a difficult time detecting what really is healthy versus unhealthy communication. I then explain the main differences of the three types of communication, just so we have a common understanding before enacting this role-play. I explain the main points of the three types of behavior as shown in the handout for T.I.P. #26. Group members usually agree with my definitions and are in fact almost bored, since they "know it already!" This gives the role-play even more impact than if this introduction were not given, as invariably there are only none to a few in any group, regardless of size, that do indeed get it "right"! This is true even among an audience of mental health professionals who already have learned these concepts!

The following basic role-play can serve as a model for your design of other role-play scenes . . .

Dinner Meeting Scene

Situation: A friend has a history of being late for dinner engagements with you. You have been increasingly upset about this. On this occasion, your friend is 20 minutes late, and you decide to say something finally, since you are very upset and feel disrespected.

Friend: Hi. What's up?

Facilitator . . .

Friend: Oh, I hadn't noticed the time!

Facilitator . . .

Friend: You're much too sensitive. I'm not that late!

Facilitator . . .

Friend: Come on, you're being petty. I was tied up!

Facilitator . . .

Friend: You shouldn't feel that way!

Facilitator . . .

Friend: Okay. I'll try to be on time next time.

Using the above dialog, have a group participant read the canned lines and you respond first in an aggressive manner. (Suggested responses for the role-plays are demonstrated in T.I.P.s #23 through #25.) For example, after the role-play where I am clearly aggressive (T.I.P. #23), I ask the group to commit to an opinion and write down which type of behavior was shown. Then I ask them to write down how the other person behaved in response to this. Invariably in the first scene where I am aggressive, most view me as being assertive, and often view the group volunteer reading the canned lines as also assertive or non-assertive. I ask that they write their answers down because when I just ask for a show of hands, participants often change their minds according to group pressure. After the show of hands, I tell them to their surprise that we were both actually very aggressive and then proceed to explain why. Line-by-line ideas are shown in T.I.P.s #23 through #25, and T.I.P. #26 is a handout describing the three types of behavior.

PROCESSING: This is one of the most powerful, relevant, and perspective-altering exercises that I use in a group setting. Because most people in groups or workshops do not differentiate accurately between the three types of communication and guess incorrectly, they often are all ears for hearing the explanation of how I was being aggressive. If I had demonstrated the role-play and then simply told them how I was behaving, they would tend to be Monday morning quarterbacks—ready with an after-the-fact obvious answer. Thus, the order of this role-play activity is very important. People have approached me years later to tell me how that exercise and accompanying handout had life changing effects on their marriages, their relationships with family members, and so on. Notice that in all three scenes, the friend's lines remain the same. All too often people think they can act according to the way others act; this role-play activity demonstrates that you do not have to stoop to someone's level. Rather, if the other person has rude things to say, you still can act with class and assertiveness. Contrary to popular belief, no one can make us act any way at all! This exercise can be an important component of a DBT group during the Assertive Skills component of the group experience, as assertiveness is an important feature in the life skills training focus of the DBT group experience.

AGGRESSIVE ROLE-PLAY SCENARIO

Dinner Meeting Scene

Situation: A friend has a history of being late for dinner engagements with you. You have been increasingly upset. This time, your friend is 20 minutes late, and you decide to say something finally, since you are very upset and feel disrespected.

Friend: Hi. What's up?

Facilitator: I've been ready for 20 minutes now. Where have you been? (rhetorical question)

Friend: Oh, I hadn't noticed the time!

Facilitator: You should be wearing a watch! (telling friend how to dress)

Friend: You're much too sensitive. I'm not that late!

Facilitator: How can you say that? (another rhetorical question) We'll be 20 minutes late now!

Friend: Come on, you're being petty. I was tied up!

Facilitator: I think you're being petty—20 minutes is a lot of time to be late. (Notice the labeling and name calling.)

Friend: You shouldn't feel that way!

Facilitator: You shouldn't tell me how I should feel! (Notice the double "should"—she "should" on me once, I "should" on her twice . . . nah, nah, nah, nah!)

Friend: Okay. I'll try to be on time next time.

Facilitator: Thanks, I appreciate it!

Note: Notice the "you" focus in the responses. Rhetorical questions are meant to put someone on the spot. In this example, two friends are "shoulding" on each other. "Shoulds" are aggressive statements and imply criticism and judgment.

NON-ASSERTIVE ROLE-PLAY SCENARIO

Dinner Meeting Scene

Situation: A friend has a history of being late for dinner engagements with you. You have been increasingly upset. This time, your friend is 20 minutes late, and you decide to say something finally, since you are very upset and feel disrespected.

Friend: Hi. What's up?

Facilitator: Oh, you got here! Oh, hi!

Friend: Oh, I hadn't noticed the time!

Facilitator: No big deal; it's only 20 minutes or so. (You are being dishonest, since according to the role-play instructions, you are upset.)

Friend: You're much too sensitive. I'm not that late!

Facilitator: I guess you're right. You can see I am upset. I'm just a stickler for time. (putting self down)

Friend: Come on, you're being petty. I was tied up!

Facilitator: Sorry, I just kind of like to be on time. (apologizing for how you feel!)

Friend: You shouldn't feel that way!

Facilitator: I know. I wish I was not such a stickler. Maybe it's my obsessive compulsiveness showing. HA! (laughing at oneself and labeling oneself)

Friend: Okay. I'll try to be on time next time.

Facilitator: Thanks.

ASSERTIVE ROLE-PLAY SCENARIO

Dinner Meeting Scene

Situation: A friend has a history of being late for dinner engagements with you. You have been increasingly upset. This time, your friend is 20 minutes late, and you decide to say something finally, since you are very upset and feel disrespected.

Friend: Hi. What's up?

Facilitator: I've been waiting for you for 20 minutes. I was getting annoyed!

Friend: Oh, I hadn't noticed the time!

Facilitator: I would appreciate you making an effort to be on time. I feel uncomfortable holding the table so long when there are people waiting. (Notice the "I" focus.)

Friend: You're much too sensitive. I'm not that late!

Facilitator: I just wanted to let you know how I feel. I just feel uncomfortable. (again, not focusing or being judgmental of the other person)

Friend: Come on, you're being petty. I was tied up!

Facilitator: It has happened a few times before, and I just wanted to let you know how I feel.

Friend: You shouldn't feel that way!

Facilitator: That is the way I feel. (repeats the same message, in a matter of fact manner—no need to explain)

Friend: Okay. I'll try to be on time next time.

Facilitator: Thanks.

Note: Point out the "I" statements and "I" focus, despite the aggressive lines from the friend.

Judith A. Belmont, M.S. (2006) • *The Therapeutic Toolbox: 103 Group Activities and T.I.P.S.* • www.worksiteinsights.com • All rights reserved.

ASSERTIVE, AGGRESSIVE, AND NON-ASSERTIVE BEHAVIOR

Assertive

Respectful of others
Honest, but tactful
Sincere
Self-confident
"I'm okay; you're okay."
Using "I" statements
Nonjudgmental
Supportive

Aggressive

"I'm okay; you're not!"
Judgmental
Domineering
"Shoulds" on self and others
Critical
Honest at someone else's
   expense
One-upmanship
Sarcastic humor

Non-Assertive

"You're okay; I'm not."
Self-demeaning
Feels like a "martyr"
Wants to be accepted
Avoidant
Needs to be liked
Lets others choose
Does not take responsibility

Payoff and Effects

Self-confidence
Freedom in relationships
Does not "get back at" others
Does not build up tension
Self-accepting
Accepting of others

Payoff and Effects

Feels superior
Gets needs met in short term
Might be guilty and alienated
Isolated
Feels mighty
Wants to be "right"

Payoff and Effects

Avoids conflict
Others don't "get mad" at them
Does not make waves
Accumulates tension and
   anger
Does not hurt feelings
"Safe"—Doesn't change

Layman Terms

Classy
Poised
Kind
Good natured
Mature

Layman Terms

Bully
Arrogant
Bossy
Intolerant
"Know it all"

Layman Terms

Wimp
Doormat
Coward
Passive
Timid

T.I.P. #27
GROUP ROLE-PLAY: TOOLS IN PRACTICE (T.I.P.) CARDS

THEORY: This exercise is an excellent example of how concepts in this T.I.P.s workbook can be put directly into practice. In a group situation, after addressing the three types of communication, skills can be cemented through use of these Tools In Practice cards. Giving group participants hands-on practice in identifying the three types of communication can provide lifelong tools.

IMPLEMENTATION: With these T.I.P. cards, members take turns reading aloud a card and having others in the group guess which type of communication is being portrayed. On the top left corner of the card is the answer, so the individual can match the verbal with the non-verbal message. They can ham up their portrayal of being non-assertive or aggressive, and this often provides the group some comic relief! If desired, cards pertaining to any group's specific issues can be made on 3 by 5 cards.

PROCESSING: People see themselves in the various types of T.I.P. cards, and this leads to a sense of universality that others have the same habits of thinking and communicating. This exercise involves the entire group and can take as little as ten minutes or as long as an hour, depending on how much discussion you wish to pursue.

T.I.P. CARDS

Aggressive "I think you stink!"	Non-Assertive (Clams up in fear of being yelled at)
Aggressive "You see? If you listened you would have known that!"	Non-Assertive *"I am really sorry but I can't help you out because I have to drive the kids to their friends' houses, and then I have to go to the store to get some groceries, and since we are leaving next weekend I have to start getting packed . . ."*
Assertive "I can't help you out today— I feel very overwhelmed right now."	Non-Assertive "Do you, umm, think it would be okay for me maybe to try that?"
Aggressive "Why do you act that way?"	Assertive "I don't think that I am getting my point across to you."

Aggressive "I should have expected that from you!"	Non-Assertive "I'm not very good at anything, really."
Aggressive "How many times do I have to tell you to put those safety glasses on?"	Aggressive "You should know better!"
Aggressive "You always do that!"	Non-Assertive "I know I shouldn't feel that way."
Non-Assertive "I know I am way too sensitive"	Make your own example.

T.I.P. #28
GROUP ROLE-PLAY: OPEN-ENDED TOOLS IN PRACTICE (T.I.P.) CARDS

THEORY: These Tools In Practice cards are less structured than those in T.I.P. #27, in that the whole sentence is not given; rather, the group member must make up a response based on an open-ended issue on the card. This is a more advanced version than the other and often is used after the group has become comfortable with the previous T.I.P. activity. Here participants can try out skills and cement them by putting them into practice.

IMPLEMENTATION: These cards contain the beginning of a sentence or just an idea, and the participant responds in one of the three styles of communication. Then others in the group guess whether the response was assertive, non-assertive, or aggressive. There is much room in this activity for people to ham it up, so comic relief is a common byproduct. If desired, you can create cards to relate to the issues of particular group members or group themes. In order to encourage whole-group participation, each person in the group should have at least one turn.

PROCESSING: These open-ended note cards spur much discussion, as the differences in the three types of communication behavior are not always so clear-cut. In addition, the non-verbal behaviors are thrown into the mix. Participants get to practice skills, or learn by exaggerating ineffective behavior. Invariably participants have examples from their own lives that are prompted by these cards, and "real life" role-play situations may follow the "canned" cards.

OPEN-ENDED T.I.P. CARDS

Your spouse or child says "All you ever think about is yourself." You say . . .

A co-worker compliments you on a job well done. You really don't think you did such a great job. You say . . .

Your 8-year-old talks back to you. You say . . .

Your parent criticizes your style of dress. You say . . .

Your spouse blames you for making her/him so mad. You say . . .

You really want to ask for a raise and say . . .

A parent says to an adult child, "I'm so glad you called your brother; you have been maturing!" You respond . . .

Someone is telling you that you are not listening to her, and you respond . . .

58

T.I.P.s #29–#32
ACTIVITIES ADDRESSING NON-VERBAL COMMUNICATION

THEORY: It has been generally accepted that at least 80 percent of communication is non-verbal. Thus, even though we often are so preoccupied with what we say, it is often how we say it that conveys our true message! Non-verbal behaviors such as tone of voice, facial expression, and body posture all give impressions of how we feel about ourselves and others. When others "can't put [their] finger on" something that bothers them about another person's behavior, it might be the less tangible non-verbal communication that is being "heard" loud and clear.

T.I.P. #29 Activity: Communicating Without Saying a Word

T.I.P. #30 Activity: Handshake, Anyone?

T.I.P. #31 Activity: It's All in How You Say It!

T.I.P. #32 Activity: I Never Said He Stole the Check!

T.I.P. #29 IMPLEMENTATION: After learning the differences between the three types of communication behaviors, try instructing the group to sit in a way that is assertive, then nonassertive, and then aggressive. The non-assertive posture might include looking down, fidgeting, slumping, and so on. The aggressive behavior might include leaning forward and glaring. Even saying nothing—giving the silent treatment—is a very powerful form of communication. Then ask group members to sit assertively. (I like to add, "just like you all normally do!")

T.I.P. #30 IMPLEMENTATION: A fun way to introduce the concept of the importance of non-verbal communication is by doing a handshaking exercise. Just with firmness of grip and good eye contact one can exude assertiveness, whereas a limp handshake with eyes looking away denotes insecurity, fear, and non-assertiveness. Ask people, "Have you ever shaken hands with a dead fish?" You'll likely get a lot of groans of acknowledgment. "How about someone who takes your hand and owns it for a moment?" Have people take turns shaking hands being the "dead fish." Then take turns doing an aggressive handshake. Then shake hands assertively. These activities are usually lighthearted experiences; expect a lot of laughter.

T.I.P. #31 IMPLEMENTATION: Tone of voice is of utmost importance. You can say the same thing twice, but depending on how you express yourself, it will take on two different meanings. For example, I demonstrate how I would respond if asked if I had a nice day. If I say with a scowl looking down, "Oh, yeah; I had a great day," the message is clear that the day was NOT good! The manner of my vocal tone would reveal that I was not a happy camper, despite my choice of words. This exercise sensitizes participants to the fact that how we say things is as or more important than what we say.

T.I.P. #32 IMPLEMENTATION: This is a very powerful way to demonstrate that tone of voice almost completely determines the message. Write the line, "I never said he stole the check!" Each time through the sentence, emphasize a different word and see how different the message is each time—this helps group members realize the importance of tone and inflection and other non-verbal behaviors. When one says, "I only said . . .", remember inflection and tone are often more important than the words. Directions: Have group members take turns emphasizing each word in the sentence below. For example, the first person reads the line emphasizing "I," and group members decide what that emphasis implies.

First Person: "**I** never said he stole the check!" (Person implies someone else said it; "not me!")

Second Person: "I **never** said he stole the check." (Individual emphatically denies it.)

Third Person: "I never **said** he stole the check." (implied, thought it, but did not say it)

Fourth Person: "I never said **he** stole the check." (someone else perhaps)

Fifth Person: "I never said he **stole** the check." (borrowed, embezzled)

Sixth Person: "I never said he stole the **check**." (Course not; he stole something else!)

PROCESSING: These exercises are simple, quick, and a lot of fun for group participants. Through humor and "hamming it up," they learn important concepts of the importance of non-verbal messages in our communication. Individuals learn the importance of matching non–verbal behaviors and tone of voice with words. Women in particular at times claim they have been taught to handshake demurely and with this exercise resolve to break that habit for good! However, perhaps the most powerful exercise in this set is the "I never said he stole the check" scenario. Participants are amazed that by a mere vocal inflection, a whole new meaning can evolve from even one sentence! Group members leave this experience appreciating the power of non-verbal communication. It's not what you say but how you say it!

T.I.P. #33
ACTIVITY: TAKING A COMPLIMENT IN STRIDE

THEORY: Many group participants admit that they find it difficult to take a compliment assertively. Sometimes due to a judgmental upbringing, people are carrying around internalized messages such as "don't be selfish" and "think of others not yourself." Thus, when given a compliment, it is not unusual to feel embarrassed and to undermine the complimentor for complimenting! This exercise enlightens group members as to how they take and give compliments, and gives them feedback on how it comes across when compliments are not taken well. It also helps them learn to be more comfortable receiving compliments.

IMPLEMENTATION: This exercise is done in a group, where everyone has a chance to go around the circle and give one another a compliment. There are a couple ways to do this. The recipient can take the compliment non-assertively, and then go around again and take it aggressively, and then assertively. Or, if it is a large group, have just a few group members demonstrate and, if time allows, have members break into small groups to personalize this exercise in pairs. Even though people are just "role-playing," it is interesting to witness how many people still shrug off the compliment. In these cases, it might take repeating the role-play a few times until each group member can take a compliment assertively.

PROCESSING: This exercise can be fun and can be an eye-opener for people in getting feedback on how they come across. Discuss the reasons why it is difficult to take a compliment, and also discuss the importance of giving compliments. How did the compliment feel to give? How did it feel to receive? Which was easier? This exercise throws out the notion that it is selfish to think highly of oneself and helps people express and receive positive emotions while feeling "worthy."

T.I.P. #34
GROUP ROLE-PLAYS: CHOOSE YOUR OWN ADVENTURE

THEORY: Canned role-plays, as in T.I.P.s #23 through #25, are effective in demonstrating the three types of communication behavior, but now it is time to put them into practice! In this activity, participants come to group prepared to share and role-play an assertive scenario. With this activity, each individual gets an opportunity to tailor the learning to his/her own life and gets feedback on how he/she is coming across.

IMPLEMENTATION: When group members come prepared with a written description of their unique situation posing an assertive dilemma, expect a lively and involved session. This activity can be executed in different ways. They might come prepared with canned lines for someone else to play the other person in the role-play, or they simply can read or describe the scenario and instruct another group member on how the role should be played without having formal lines. After enacting a role-play, a participant gets feedback from group members on how he/she came across. Group members as well as the leader can point out what behaviors were effective and make suggestions to improve assertive behavior. Use the handout from T.I.P. #26 as a basis for discerning between assertive, aggressive, and non-assertive communication.

PROCESSING: These experiential role-plays, with the benefits of group experience and feedback, provide valuable insights into how one comes across to others. Clients learn just as much from the role-plays of other group members as from their own. Participants truly learn hands-on skills that can last a lifetime!

T.I.P.s #35 & #36
VIDEOTAPING IN GROUPS: READY, SET, ACTION!

THEORY: It is one thing to talk about communication skills, another to role-play enactments inspired by real life, but totally another thing to see for yourself how you come across to the world. With today's video technology, it has become easier to use this medium as a tool to learn about oneself and others.

T.I.P. #35 Videotaping Role-Plays

T.I.P. #36 Videotaping Psychoeducational Lessons

T.I.P. #35 IMPLEMENTATION: After the group has learned the differences among the three types of communication in T.I.P.s #23 through #26, and has used role-play in the group setting, the next step is to video-tape additional role-plays. Members can bring their own scenarios that they wish to role-play in session. Alternatively, each group member can be videotaped before group in a role-play with you; then the videotapes can be played in session so that the group can view the role-plays with fresh eyes. This enables people to see for themselves their non-verbal communication as well as their behaviors. Have members give constructive suggestions and feedback, including what they liked most about how the person presented himself/herself.

T.I.P. #36 IMPLEMENTATION: Another creative use of videotaping is to have the videotape roll for a portion or all of a group session and then play it back later to analyze together the communication among group members. Additionally, Marsha Linehan, in her DBT groups, suggests that tapes of group sessions be made available in between sessions (more practical of course in a residential or inpatient facility) so clients can have more time to digest the psychoeducational lessons in the group. This suggestion is less about dissecting interaction styles than it is for educational purposes and cementing the learning of that week's group lesson.

PROCESSING: Once people get over the initial adjustment of seeing themselves on video, the benefits of observing and dissecting the behavior of self and others is invaluable. Invariably people at first do not like the way they look, but as time goes on get desensitized to the self-consciousness of seeing themselves. Whether you use this tool as a way to reinforce psychoeducational concepts in the life skills portion of a DBT group, or as a vehicle to give people more insight into how they come across to others, the videotape experience potentially packs potentially packs a wallop of insight into the group experience!

QUOTES CONCERNING DIFFICULT PEOPLE

"We have two ears and one mouth so that we can listen twice as much as we speak."

—Epictetus

* * *

"Conflict cannot survive without your participation."

—Wayne Dyer

* * *

"Whenever there is a conflict between human rights and property rights, human rights must prevail."

—Abraham Lincoln

* * *

"I don't like that man. I must get to know him better."

—Abraham Lincoln

* * *

"Whenever you're in conflict with someone, there is one factor that can make the difference between damaging your relationship and deepening it. That factor is attitude."

—William James

5

Difficult People Made Easy!

T.I.P. #37
ACTIVITY: HOW DO YOU DEAL WITH BULLYING? USE FOG!

THEORY: All too often people "fight fire with fire" in the area of interpersonal communication. If someone is critical with them, they tend to lash back. This group exercise gives a hands-on example of how to be in control and diffuse aggressiveness while maintaining your composure—a great way to avoid arguments! Stop the vicious cycle; replace criticism and retaliation with fogging.

IMPLEMENTATION: Teach the group about fogging in the following mini-lecture lesson:

Fogging deflects negativity and judgmental criticism by agreeing with someone in theory but retaining the right to choose your behavior.

Fogging allows you to unhook from criticism on a gut level and to listen. At the same time, fogging allows the other person to feel heard. By fogging, you also exhaust your critic. It takes more energy than most people have to continue criticizing someone who won't react.

Stock phrases to use in fogging include: "That could be true," "You're probably right," and "Sometimes I think so myself." Remember, you are not agreeing to change your behavior—just agreeing with the possibility that the other person may be right.

Examples may sound like the following:

> *Friend:* You really should not do that!
>
> *You:* Well, maybe you have a point there!
>
> *Parent:* That shirt is much too tight!
>
> *You:* I agree. The style is for shirts to be looser nowadays.

Break into pairs and ask clients to role-play a real-life issue using "fogging."

PROCESSING: This example and mini-lesson offer life skills training and empowerment from the truth that others do not have to set the tone for your behavior.

T.I.P. #38
ROLE-PLAY: "BULLY BUSTING" WITH FOGGING

THEORY: This group role-play is a terrific way to show that no one has to push you around anymore! The harder one tries to stop an aggressor, the more the aggressive person is rewarded for his/her aggression. This lesson teaches that no one has to "get your goat!" The fogging exercise takes power away from the aggressor and teaches valuable life skills for dealing with conflict. This activity is similar to Izzy Kalman's "Izzy's Game" in his book *Bullies to Buddies*, where he uses a similar concept to diffuse aggressive situations.

IMPLEMENTATION: In group, ask a volunteer to come up and say rude things to you. Allow the volunteer to hurl insults, and initially be defensive and hurl insults back (being gentle of course!). Then ask the group if your defiance and yelling back were effective. There will be a resounding "no!" Point out that you gave the "bully" way too much power and in fact showed a lack of personal self-control, stooping to the bully's level. Point out that you basically escalated the aggression.

Now have the same person hurl the same insults, but this time say things such as, "you really think so?" "Interesting!" "I'll have to think about that." "Perhaps you have a point." It then becomes no fun for the bully, and the demonstration ends because there is nothing left to say! Review the fogging lesson after the demonstration to bring home the fact that this way of handling bullying serves to disarm the aggressor and diffuse the confrontation.

PROCESSING: Have the group brainstorm how to use fogging in real-life situations. Underscore the fact that you are not "giving in" but rather are not giving the aggressor power over you by maintaining your cool behavior. This is very powerful in a group setting, as the ineffectiveness of meeting fire with fire is readily apparent.

T.I.P. #39
ACTIVITY: DEALING WITH THE BULLY WITHIN

THEORY: We not only confront the bullies on the outside, but we often struggle with bullies in our own minds. These bullies nag, critique, judge, and put us down, and those messages we carry around undermine our sense of self-esteem and security. Fighting the bully within is an important undertaking if we want to keep a lid on the wellspring of self-doubt and critical messages that hinder our emotional well-being. This exercise was gleaned from Thom Rutledge, author of *Embracing Fear, Finding Courage,* who developed this role-play for groups and impacted PESI seminar participants with these very powerful exercises.

IMPLEMENTATION: Have group members write down three to five "inner bully messages" that hamper their sense of well-being. These might be the "shoulds" and labels they received from others in their past or present. Ask members to then place their name before each item. These messages to self might look like the following: "Jill, you are a loser and will never amount to anything" or "Bob, you have been a bad parent." Caution that these items must be ones that members are willing to share in group. After allowing a few minutes for this task, break into groups of 3 or 4. Have one person read another person's items one at a time, looking directly at the person whose list is being read. This is a very powerful exercise, as one is hearing one's "internal tape" out loud rather than hearing it only as rambling, nagging inner "self-talk." Each of the 3 or 4 group members gives the messages to and receives the messages from another member. Process in a small group as well as the large group how it felt giving and receiving the messages.

PROCESSING: Often group participants are appalled at the extreme and critical bullies that lurk in their co-members' heads. They feel guilty saying it, and feel even worse telling others than hearing their own. This is a powerful exercise; be prepared for tears and emotion. Never leave this exercise without following it up with T.I.P. #40, where one focuses on designing nurturing messages from within.

T.I.P. #40
ACTIVITY: ALLOWING THE NURTURER WITHIN "IN"!

THEORY: Group members feel relieved not to end on the negative note of T.I.P. #39, so it is strongly suggested that this always be a follow-up to T.I.P. #39. After hearing the appalling messages that people feed themselves, it is a relief to be able to hear nurturing and soothing self-statements. In his PESI workshop, Thom Rutledge, author of *Embracing Fear, Finding Courage*, followed up T.I.P. #39 with this one.

IMPLEMENTATION: This is a much kinder, gentler version of the previous exercise. This time, ask group members to write only positive, nurturing messages that can even be ideally positive and exaggerated soothing messages from an "inner nurturer." Ask members to give themselves these messages even if they do not fully embrace or believe them. Examples: "Debbie, you are someone to be really proud of!" and "Jack, you are so wonderful in your work with your clients!" Take turns as before reading them one at time in the same small groups. Have the small group and then the large group process this activity.

PROCESSING: In my experiences with this activity, we all notice that the negative messages were absolute, whereas the kinder messages seemed less extreme and, if anything, too humble!

T.I.P. #41
BULLY BUTTONS—COVERING THE BUTTONS OF VULNERABILITY

THEORY: Our "buttons" are often too exposed, and we let others push them. I introduce this topic by stating that "no one can make you upset; you allow a person to." In seeing what vulnerable "buttons" we each possess, we better understand how we often leave ourselves at others' mercy. This handout helps one feel more empowered by knowing what "buttons" one might need to work on covering!

T.I.P. #41 Handout: Bully Buttons!

IMPLEMENTATION: Have group members fill out the "Bully Buttons!" handout in either a written or verbal manner. You may have members take the handout home as a self-help assignment or work on it together in group. This activity is appropriate for children as well as adults, as concepts are presented simply.

PROCESSING: Brainstorm with group members how they can "cover" those buttons. Discuss situations where they feel a lack of control and focus on what they need to do to take more control over their own reactions. The concept that no one can make you feel a certain way is not a new one but is very difficult for many to keep in mind in their everyday patterns of thinking.

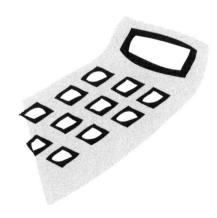

BULLY BUTTONS!

No one can make us angry; we are in charge of our anger! People do not have to push your buttons! Do not make them so accessible! Ideally, they are only yours to push!

DIRECTIONS: Write below the "buttons" that we allow others to push that cause us emotional distress. Then write how you can change your usual response.

Buttons of Vulnerability

EXAMPLE: *I am so angry when my mother makes a comment about my weight.*

Changed Response: _____

_____

MY EXAMPLE: _____

Changed Response: _____

_____

MY EXAMPLE: _____

Changed Response: _____

_____

MY EXAMPLE: _____

Changed Response: _____

_____

T.I.P. #42
ROLE-PLAY: THE FOUR GOALS OF DIFFICULT BEHAVIORS IN ACTION

THEORY: This role-play is a very fun way to demonstrate the four goals of difficult behavior in a way that group members will not likely forget! This demonstration helps clients identify the four goals (primarily unconscious to both perpetrator and recipient) of difficult behavior.

IMPLEMENTATION: Before anyone knows the four types or is given the handouts in T.I.P. #43, I ask group participants to try to get me to pick up some pens on the floor or table. I tell them they can be as aggressive as they want and promise their behavior will not be critiqued or observed. Group members are urged to observe instead what they think the underlying unconscious goal of my defiant behavior might be. The role-play often goes something like this:

First Goal Scenario

Group: Pick that up now!

Facilitator: No. You're not my mother! I don't have to listen to you!

Group: Come on. Just pick them up; there are only a few.

Facilitator: I don't have to!

Group: Now, when you pick them up we can play with the clay.

Facilitator: Make me!

(At this point, I stop the role-play—"CUT!" I then ask the group what my goal was. What is the goal? "POWER" or "CONTROL.")

For demonstration purposes for this book, I will show typical answers from the three other major goals:

Second Goal Scenario

Group: Pick that up now!

Facilitator: Why should I? You didn't help me last week when I asked you!

Group: Come on. Just pick them up; there are only a few.

Facilitator: Why didn't you help me last week then?

Group: Now, when you pick them up we can play with the clay.

Facilitator: Maybe next time you'll be more considerate!

(At this point, I stop the role-play—"CUT!" I then ask the group what my goal was. What is the goal? "REVENGE.")

Third Goal Scenario

Group: Pick that up now!

Facilitator: Look at how pretty the pens are!

Group: Come on. Just pick them up; there are only a few.

Facilitator: Which color do you like best?

Group: Now, when you pick them up we can play with the clay.

Facilitator: They are pretty pens, don't you think?

(At this point I stop the role-play—"CUT!" I then ask the group what my goal was. What is the goal? "ATTENTION." How often someone acts difficult in order to get attention and be noticed!)

Fourth Goal Scenario

Group: Pick that up now!

Facilitator: It's so hard!

Group: Come on. Just pick them up; there are only a few.

Facilitator: I'm tired!

Group: Now, when you pick them up we can play with the clay.

Facilitator: You're better than I am at doing that.

(At this point I stop the role-play—"CUT!" I then ask the group what my goal was. What is the goal? "DISPLAY OF INADEQUACY." How often someone's obnoxiousness is a quest to control others!)

PROCESSING: Make the point that the goals of misbehavior are not often in the range of conscious awareness. These four role-play scenarios and the lessons they teach can explain why children do poorly at school, why couples argue about things they cannot remember the following day, why some people don't even try, and why others try too hard to change others. Help clients be detectives as to the reasons "behind the scenes"!

T.I.P. #43
DEALING WITH DIFFICULT BEHAVIOR: THE FOUR GOALS

THEORY: In reading the various *Systematic Training for Effective Parenting* (STEP) books, originally by the father-son Dinkmeyer team, one of the best lessons I learned was not only an understanding of parenting skills but also an understanding of the four goals of difficult behavior among all people, regardless of age. Though *The Parent's Handbook: Systematic Training for Effective Parenting* (STEP) (McKay & Dinkmeyer, Sr.) focuses on children's difficult behavior, these concepts apply to people of all ages. I have challenged many clients, both individuals and in groups to find a fifth goal of difficult behavior, but no other goal has been found! Insight into the four main goals of difficult behavior has shed light on marital dysfunction, co-worker struggles, and difficulties with family members. Understanding and identifying the four goals can help us be less controlled by the difficult behavior of others.

T.I.P. #43 Handout: Goals of Difficult Behavior

T.I.P. #43 Handout: Four Goals of Difficult Behavior

IMPLEMENTATION: I first give group members the following two-page handout based on the STEP chart of the four goals of difficult behavior. I ask the group to dissect a conflict-ridden interpersonal situation and then try to identify the goal of the other person's difficult behavior. Of course, these goals are not generally conscious goals. In understanding the unconscious motivations behind conflict, it is easier first to forgive the person for the misbehavior, as it helps one distance oneself and makes it less likely that one will be enmeshed in the drama any longer. This concept is especially powerful in a marital session where blame then can be bypassed, the need to be right can diminish in importance, and a more rational and objective manner of handling the other can take center stage.

PROCESSING: Many people find that identifying the goals makes difficult situations more manageable, and helps demystify the confusing and challenging behaviors of others, as well as themselves!

GOALS OF DIFFICULT BEHAVIOR

GOAL	BELIEF	WAYS TO DEAL WITH THE BEHAVIOR
ATTENTION	I want to be noticed. I like being the "center of attention." If people notice me, then I feel like "somebody."	Ignore the behavior. Do not let others manipulate you! Refuse to enable.
POWER	I have ideas of how I want others to be. I have strong feelings of the way things should be. I feel best when I am "in control." No one can boss me around or take advantage.	Don't overpower. Forgive the bullying. Remain assertive. Do not let someone violate your rights.
REVENGE	If someone does this to me, they deserve this behavior! They started it! If someone hurts me, they are going to get hurt too. Tit for tat! I've been hurt in the past.	Do not take things personally. It matters "who ends it." Forgive the person for being unhealthy. Do not let someone push your buttons! Do not retaliate!
DISPLAY OF INADEQUACY	I'm a loser! I'm helpless. It does not matter how I act I can't change! I can't help it! I've always been this way! You can't fail or get hurt if you don't try.	Express compassion. Encourage. This is really a choice. Show respect for self and others. Don't pity. Suspend judgmental thinking.

(Adapted from G. D. McKay & D. C. Dinkmeyer, Sr. [1989]. *The Parent's Handbook: Systematic Training for Effective Parenting* [STEP]. Circle Pines, MN: American Guidance Service.)

FOUR GOALS OF DIFFICULT BEHAVIOR

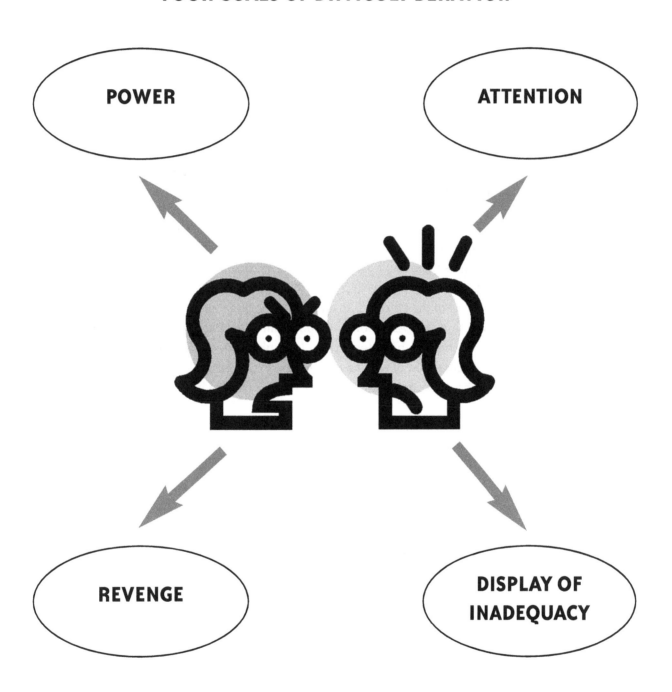

(Adapted from Dinkemeyer & Dinkmeyer, *The Parent's Handbook: Systematic Training for Effective Parenting.*)

T.I.P. #44
THE INVISIBLE SHIELD

THEORY: In the midst of interpersonal interactions, here is another way to guard against allowing someone to "push your buttons." This exercise makes people aware that they do not have to let someone "make" them feel a certain way. This serves as a visual reminder that people have control over themselves if they keep their messages clearly in front of them—literally!

IMPLEMENTATION: This activity requires a large piece of Plexiglas. Also have handy a pad of sticky notes. Brainstorm with group members what sticky note messages they can think of that will help them think clearly when dealing with someone who is bullying. The Plexiglas serves as an invisible shield between them and the "aggressor." Give the group a few minutes to write messages that can be seen only by them and not the bully. Put the Plexiglas up and invite a group member to put his/her messages on the Plexiglas facing toward him/her. Ask another group member act like the real-life "bully," and have the two then role-play with the help of the notes on the "invisible barrier." Sample messages include: "I don't have to answer him," "I am proud of who I am," "He has no power to make me feel any way," "Who owns the problem?" and "If he does something irrational, I will not accept blame or responsibility."

PROCESSING: Although these messages might be obvious on the surface, this is a great example and demonstration of how we can have an "Invisible Shield" between ourselves and a bully. Using Plexiglas with sticky notes shows us that there is not a direct line to the bully at all. It is up to us to intercept messages to soften a bully's blow.

T.I.P. #45
TREATMENT RESISTANCE: IT'S JUST THE TIP OF THE ICEBERG!

THEORY: Treatment resistance and defiance in groups is common, especially when people are mandated to attend groups. Typical phrases one might hear are "I don't know" and "I don't care." Of course, this happens in one-on-one counseling also, but this activity is very powerful in a group setting, especially with group input. I have used this technique with adolescent groups in schools that were mandated to participate in an anger management group.

IMPLEMENTATION: When there are various attempts to close off group processing through inappropriate comments and statements, the iceberg example is a great way to get group members to give up the habit! An iceberg (facilitator's guide is shown on the next page) is put on the chalkboard or flipchart, with counterproductive words that you often hear in group—in this case, "I don't know" and "I don't care." Ask group members what is really behind these statements. In order not to have people feel put on the spot, I suggest that they think of why someone (but it doesn't necessarily have to be them) would be so negative. Ask them to imagine what is going on with that person for him/her to be so resistant to the group process. There likely will be no shortage of explanations from the group. Then make a list under the water on the iceberg picture. Sample ideas are "sadness," "anger," "low self-esteem," "hurt," "feeling like no one cares about you," and so on. Finally, point to the iceberg picture and ask, "Which reasons describe you?" (After this exercise, group members often give up extreme resistance, such as voicing the very remarks we discussed.)

PROCESSING: This dissection of resistant phrases such as "I don't know" and "I don't care" makes it difficult to get away with them any longer! No one wants to "give themselves away" or be "misunderstood," so the group shifts from negative and undermining statements to more open and positive ones!

DIFFICULT CLIENT BEHAVIOR IN GROUP THERAPY

QUOTES TO "DESTRESS FOR SUCCESS!"

"You'll never be on the top of the world if you try to carry it on your shoulders."

—Unknown

* * *

"When I look back on all these worries, I remember the story of the old man who said on his deathbed that he had had a lot of trouble in his life, most of which had never happened."

—Winston Churchill

* * *

"If you are distressed by anything external, the pain is not due to the thing itself but to your own estimate of it; and this you have the power to revoke at any moment."

—Marcus Aurelius

* * *

"Do not anticipate trouble or worry about what may never happen. Keep in the sunlight."

—Benjamin Franklin

* * *

"Stress is the spice of life."

—Hans Selye

Destress for Success!

T.I.P.s #46–#48
ACTIVITIES FOR STRESS MANAGEMENT: FROM STRESSED TO DESSERTS!

THEORY: Stress management is a vital component of any psychoeducational program. Stress is a concept that is grossly misunderstood. All too often stress gets a "bad rap." It is often regarded far too negatively. Stress can just as well be positive as negative. The trick is to get stress to work for you rather than have stress work against you! These activities introduce important concepts about stress. They provide three ways to introduce concepts about stress so that hopefully group members can become "stress managers" and not "stress carriers"!

T.I.P. #46 Activity: Stress Is . . .

T.I.P. #47 Activity: Sharing about Stress

T.I.P. #48 Mini-Lecture on Stress

T.I.P. #46 IMPLEMENTATION: On note cards, ask group participants to fill in the rest of the phrase "Stress is. . . ." Ask them to write at least five items. Next, have participants put a plus or minus by each item, depending on whether they view the item as a positive or negative stress. In going over the results, it is clear that most often, stress is seen as more negative than positive, so be sure to point out that stress can be positive also. Perhaps it is the attitude toward stress that needs to be altered.

T.I.P. #47 IMPLEMENTATION: In a group situation, you can augment the previous T.I.P. by asking participants to share their answers aloud while you write them on a flipchart or chalkboard. After they share their answers, add pluses or minuses next to each item depicting how the group as a whole views each stress (negatively or positively). Typical responses are negative—"fatigue," " too much to do," "too little time," "over-worked," "depressed," "trouble with finances," and so on. Imagine their surprise when you point out that these descriptions represent only one view of stress—distress. Stress, however, can also be very positive and is necessary in our lives. Brainstorm how we can change the negative concepts of stress to more positive ones.

T.I.P. #48 IMPLEMENTATION: The previous two activities lead well into the mini-lecture on positive and negative stress. I show a power point slide on this topic, along with the reminder that the opposite of "Stressed" is "Desserts"!

There Are
Two Types of Stress

POSITIVE STRESS

- Eustress
- Allows you to react quickly to danger
- Increased energy to deal quickly with situation
- Helps focus your attention
- Exhilaration, opportunity

NEGATIVE STRESS

- Leads to burnout
- Stress controls you
- Physical symptoms: tightness, headaches, illness, dizziness, body
- Emotional symptoms: anxiety, depression, irritability, moodiness, boredom

It's a fact! "Stressed" spelled backward is "Desserts"!

PROCESSING: These exercises are a great introduction to the subject of stress. Many are surprised that stress can indeed be positive. We all have stress—it is how we view and handle it that determines if it is harmful or helpful.

T.I.P.s #49–#52
GROUP ACTIVITIES AND MINI-LECTURES FOR STRESS MANAGEMENT

THEORY: These short, fun exercises are helpful in providing a social skills training focus, which is so vital in DBT groups as well as in any psychoeducational framework. Effective therapy often requires having tools for teaching social skills training. Here are some of my favorite props that aid group members in visualizing the delicate balance between positive and negative stress.

T.I.P. #49 Mini-Lecture on Stress Chart

T.I.P. #50 Activity: Stretching for Stress!

T.I.P. #51 Stress Activity with Strings Attached

T.I.P #52 Stress Activity Inflated

T.I.P. #49 IMPLEMENTATION: Share the stress chart shown below on a flipchart or chalkboard. On the bell-shaped curve, one extreme represents too little stress, which leads to boredom, apathy, lack of involvement, and loneliness. The other extreme represents feeling too much pressure and anxiety. In the middle, however, is the delicate balance for which we all strive.

In control, alive, involved, vibrant

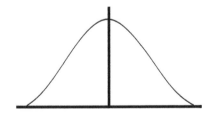

loneliness
boredom
apathy
lack of involvement

nervous breakdown,
pressure
anxiety, panic
over-commitment

T.I.P. #50 IMPLEMENTATION: After introducing the stress chart in T.I.P. #49, take a rubber-band and stretch it out. Point out that this is how people feel when they are "stressed out" and overwhelmed. Then leave it limp—too little stress makes one feel bored, depressed, and uninvolved. Now, stretch it half way—it has form, function, and purpose, which is a symbol of achieving a work–life balance. The goal in life is to find the optimal level of stress. People can apply this visual exercise to their own lives. If they are overworked and overcommitted, they might feel as if they will "snap." Too little involvement, however, makes one "limp" and without zest. Finding the right balance can help one to feel involved and "in charge." Give everyone a rubber-band and have them show how they feel today in terms of their stress level.

T.I.P. #51 IMPLEMENTATION: You can liken stress to the string of a musical instrument: If the string is tuned too tightly, it pops. If it is not tightened enough, it sounds flat. Only the optimum amount of tightening produces beautiful music! You might have as a prop a guitar or string instrument, and you or a volunteer can make the sound either drone or play beautiful music depending on the level of "stress."

T.I.P. #52 IMPLEMENTATION: A balloon is another great visual example to show that stress management is a balancing act. Give all group members a balloon and have them blow them up to the point of how stressed they felt that morning. Then, ask them to show how they feel now. You might ask them to go around and share what situations make them feel limp and others that make them feel ready to pop. In all the variations, just caution them not to have it pop in their face!

PROCESSING: Visuals and active exercises are a great way for people to have fun and feel part of an experiential process without being "on the spot" or threatened. People generally enjoy these visual images, and hands-on experiences bring home the concept that stress is necessary and deserves more respect than is generally given. The point is successfully demonstrated in these activities that stress can be a friend as part of a healthy lifestyle balance—as long as it does not backfire!

T.I.P.s #53 & #54
STRESS EMERGENCY KIT: DON'T LEAVE HOME WITHOUT IT!

THEORY: We have "emergency kits" for medical needs. Why not stress kits for mental health needs? This activity is a fun and very visual way to help people develop creative thinking skills for coping with stress.

T.I.P. #53 Stress Emergency Kit

T.I.P. #54 Make Your Own Stress Emergency Kit

T.I.P. #53 IMPLEMENTATION: In this group activity, I provide group participants with plastic zip lock bags filled with items for their stress survival kit. Have participants guess what each item stands for.

Examples:

- Rubber-band (reminds you of the optimal level of stress)
- Hershey's Kiss and Hug (everyone needs a hug and kiss sometimes)
- Crayon (to color your world)
- Paintbrush (attitude is the mind's paintbrush!)
- Paperclip (helps you "hold it together"!)
- Mini ball (reminds you to play)
- Yellow smiley face stickers (reminds you to smile)
- Comic clipping (remember to laugh)
- Sticky notes (write a reminder, e.g., not to take things too personally)

T.I.P. #54 IMPLEMENTATION: Instead of having bags made up, have items from T.I.P. #53, along with others of your choice, in the middle of the table and have group members make up their own stress survival kits. You might even have magazines to cut up or a pen and file cards handy to have them draw things to represent what you have not made available to them. Then ask group members to go around presenting their kit to others, explaining what the items in their bags symbolize to them.

PROCESSING: This is a very colorful and fun group exercise. Lots of laughter and humor go along with very serious learning. This activity is perfect for a psychoeducational group, in DBT or other format. This is great for any group activity where leaders want to give clients tools to handle stress.

T.I.P. #55
ACTIVITY: STRESS FOR SUCCESS!

THEORY: This game involves active participation. All you need are stress balls to keep the game going. Whether this be used for a lesson on stress, for teambuilding, or as a group energizer, this is a wonderful hands-on activity that virtually everyone enjoys. This provides a great opportunity to experience how stress can be fun! People also like the chance to get up and move in this activity.

IMPLEMENTATION: Ask participants to stand and form circles of about five to eight people. Give each group one stress ball to begin. Have the first person throw a ball to someone else and remember who they threw it to since they will be asked to remember and continue the same pattern. If there is only one group, you can be part of the group, but if there is more than one, make sure you are not in the mix, since you will need to move around between groups. Each person throws the ball to someone who has not yet had the ball. The last person sends it back to the original person who "keeps the ball rolling" a little faster then next time. (Do not have them throw to the same person twice until all members have gotten it first.) Once they have the pattern down, introduce another ball—then another and then another. Balls drop, roll, etc., but urge them to pick them up and continue. With five or six balls going at a time, it becomes quite a circus with a lot of laughing!

PROCESSING: After about five minutes, have everyone sit down and identify what they can learn from the activity (besides it being hard to keep all the balls in the air!). What did they learn they had to do to be successful? How many thought of what they would eat for dinner, etc.? This is a great lesson on mindfulness, as people are totally in the present, and thus would be an ideal activity for DBT groups when addressing the subject of mindfulness. Point out that life is like the activity—we all juggle many things at one time, and if we are not focused, things get dropped! If we focus too much on the past or present, the stress balls will pound and bombard us if we are not alert. Note: You can order stress balls through many vendors on the internet by putting in the keyword "stress balls." (They are foam bouncing balls that are soft and will not cause injury.)

T.I.P. #56
ACTIVITY: STRESS IN A DOT— A BIODOT, THAT IS

THEORY: In a group, participants have fun looking at how "stressed" they are with "Biodots." "Biodots" can be purchased online and stick to your skin and change color according to body temperature, revealing how stressed one is. This is often accompanied with a relaxation exercise, and participants get to see what color their dot is before and after the exercise. Even if the reliability of what the colors actually mean is suspect, group members have fun with them!

IMPLEMENTATION: Biodots can be purchased online from many internet sites. You can order them in dots, squares, and uncut larger sheets to make your own shapes. Have all group members put the dot in the same spot in the top of the hand near the V between thumb and index finder. The Biodots come with a color chart to help interpret what the various shades of colors mean. Explain that these dots are meant to measure body temperature changes to detect how much stress you are feeling. Have members keep the dots on throughout the session and at times look at the color changes. Does the color change during more relaxing activities or interactions? During role-play, does the color change dramatically?

PROCESSING: In this activity, we see that body temperature is affected by stress. Whether or not the dots reveal anything meaningful is a matter of interpretation, but the activity captures universal interest as it becomes a teambuilding and icebreaking activity. You might joke with group members that you can give them extra dots to take home to prove who in their family is a "stress manager" and who is a "stress carrier"—one who deals with stress by giving it to others!

T.I.P. #57
ACTIVITY: COMPARING A STRESS BALL TO A STRESS RESILIENT PERSONALITY

THEORY: How is a stress ball like a stress resilient personality? We can learn much from the lessons of a stress ball.

IMPLEMENTATION: Ask group members how a stress resilient personality is like a stress ball. Comments commonly include: it bounces back; rolls with the punches; no hard edges; soft on the inside; when squeezed, it finds shape again.

PROCESSING: The stress ball offers a great visual for learning the many lessons that the stress ball teaches. One can learn to roll with things and learn to bounce back through life's harsh realities if one remains flexible and resilient!

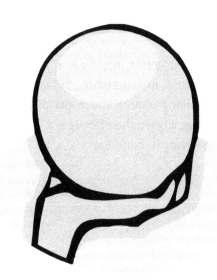

T.I.P. #58
ACTIVITY: SYMPTOMS OF INNER PEACE

THEORY: This exercise humorously depicts symptoms of inner peace. It is a tongue-in-cheek exercise about the seriousness of symptoms—like the loss of ability to criticize others! Group participants appreciate the humorous look at what one needs to give up when one gets healthier.

IMPLEMENTATION: Warn group participants that by healthier thinking patterns and handling stress better, they might feel the "serious side effects" of inner peace. On a flipchart or chalkboard ask participants to brainstorm side effects of inner peace (see facilitator's guide on the following page). Have group participants chime in and offer more items depicting the serious symptoms of inner peace.

PROCESSING: This humorous look at the side effects of inner peace can be a fun and enlightening group activity. Through generation of the list, participants embark on the serious business of seeing the lighter side of dealing effectively with stress.

SYMPTOMS OF INNER PEACE

Here are some possible items to begin with:

- A loss of interest in judging others
- Loss of the ability to worry over things out of your control
- Frequent laughing
- Criticizing others is no fun anymore
- Being right ain't what it used to be!
- The uncontrollable urge to smile frequently

Now fill in your own ideas:

_____

_____

_____

_____

_____

_____

_____

_____

_____

_____

Judith A. Belmont, M.S. *(2006)* • *The Therapeutic Toolbox: 103 Group Activities and T.I.P.S.* • www.worksiteinsights.com •

QUOTES ON CHANGE

"They say that time changes things, but you actually have to change them yourself."

—Andy Warhol

* * *

"Things do not change, we change."

—Henry David Thoreau

* * *

"You cannot step twice into the same river, for other waters are continually flowing in."

—Heraclitus (ca. 500 BCE)

* * *

"Change is the law of life. And those who look only to the past or present are certain to miss the future."

—John F. Kennedy

Changing Times

T.I.P.s #59–#62
ACTIVITIES FOR ADAPTING TO CHANGE

THEORY: These four exercises show that one needs to be resilient and open to change in developing healthy perspectives and new ways of looking at things. Instead of just talking about looking at things in a different way, bring home the point by actually shaking things up!

T.I.P. #59 Trading Places

T.I.P. #60 Technique to Deal with the Treatment Resistant Client

T.I.P. #61 Changing Roles: Empathy Building

T.I.P. #62 Changing Times

T.I.P. #59 IMPLEMENTATION: At your next group session, have everyone take all their belongings along and switch seats. Talk about how it feels—put yourself in someone else's shoes! This is great for changing perspective.

T.I.P. #60 IMPLEMENTATION: Have group members "put on a different hat" by taking turns sitting in your chair and you sitting in different group members' places. Have group members put themselves in your shoes to get more of an objective view of how they come across. (This is great for the treatment resistant client in group; it helps "turn the tables.")

T.I.P. #61 IMPLEMENTATION: A variation of these perspective altering techniques is to have all group members be the "therapist" and you be the "client." Pick a real-life situation that poses an assertiveness issue or any topic you regard as appropriate and "safe," and have the group provide you with skills and suggestions. This can be quite helpful in breaking the defensiveness of the disruptive, antisocial or narcissistic client.

T.I.P. #62 IMPLEMENTATION: Have clients put their watches on the other wrist and ask them to wear it that way until the next group meeting. Ask clients how this felt and what they can learn from that.

PROCESSING: Brainstorm how it feels to "shake things up." These four creative ways of demonstrating dealing with change offer fresh perspective and work well with even the most treatment resistant clients who are feeling stuck.

T.I.P. #63
QUOTE THERAPY ON THE SUBJECT OF CHANGE

THEORY: Quotes pack a wallop of insight into simple phrases, as is shown before each chapter in this workbook. I am using the topic of change to show how quotes can be used in the therapeutic process. Using quotes on any topic lead to powerful insights. Since treatment resistant clients often have a difficult time with change—choosing "survival" over change—here are some sample quotes you can employ as a springboard to discussion of the positive aspects of change.

IMPLEMENTATION: Share some quotes on a handout, flipchart, or power point slide. One at a time, read a quote and discuss. This is an ideal way to introduce a topic and craft the direction of the group. There are many sites on the internet that provide inspirational quotes for a variety of topics.

PROCESSING: Quotes are a very effective way to introduce the concept of change. All too often, people say they do not like change, but if a person remains stuck in non-productive patterns, a person cannot grow. But a person can learn how to embrace change with the help of inspirational messages of wisdom from our predecessors and other noteworthy individuals. Although the focus of this exercise is change, many topics will work in the same manner. Perhaps begin each group session with a quote or two that serves as a springboard for discussion relating to that day's agenda.

"Change alone is unchanging."

—Heraclitus (c. 535–c. 475 B.C.), Greek philosopher

"God, grant me the serenity to accept the things I cannot change, the courage to change the things I can, and the wisdom to know the difference."

—Reinhold Niebuhr

"They always say that time changes things, but you actually have to change them yourself.

—Andy Warhol

"We must become the change we want to see."

—Mahatma Ghandhi

T.I.P. #64
GROUP DISCUSSION: SURVIVAL OVER CHANGE

THEORY: This brainstorming activity can help group members uncover reasons they remain stuck in non-productive life patterns. One concept made very clear in Dialectical Behavioral Therapy (DBT) is that the most troubled and suicidal clients, including those with personality disorders, often remain in non-productive patterns because they have chosen "survival over change."

IMPLEMENTATION: Introduce the concept of "survival over change." Explain to the group that when one has trauma and stress in early years, one often remains stuck in unhealthy patterns of behavior in order to "survive" a toxic situation. Explain that throughout life, these patterns might become no longer adaptive, but may continue due to one's fear of change and a skills deficit. Brainstorm and write on a flipchart or board the pros and cons of changing. What does one give up to change? How does one learn to develop new skills to change? Have group participants imagine how they would be different if they were in a "change" frame of mind instead of a "survival" frame of mind.

PROCESSING: This topic for group discussion can be eye-opening for individuals who have never considered that their fear of change and difficulty in changing might be in part explained by never having fully switched from a "survival" mode to a "change" mode. This serves to validate their reasons—the notion of "no wonder you are like that; you needed to be that way to survive the trauma" can be extremely comforting. You can share with group members that an appropriate title for this discussion can be borrowed from Bob Dylan: "The Times They Are A Changin'."

QUOTES ON SELF-DISCOVERY

"Life is an endless process of self-discovery."

—James Gardner

* * *

"When you examine the lives of the most influential people who have ever walked among us, you discover one thread that winds through them all. They have been aligned first with their spiritual nature and only then with their physical selves."

—Albert Einstein

* * *

"I went to the woods because I wished to live deliberately . . . and not, when I came to die, discover that I had not lived."

—Henry David Thoreau

* * *

"Your work is to discover your world and then with all your heart give yourself to it."

—Buddha

Self-Discovery

T.I.P.s #65-#67
IMAGERY EXERCISES: THE COURTROOM AND BOARD OF DIRECTORS

THEORY: It is not uncommon for our clients to carry around critical and judgmental messages from the past that handicap self-esteem. All too commonly, clients suffer from cruel judgments that they automatically accept early in their lives and that become woven into the fabric of their core self-view. This exercise helps clients identify these messages and examine whether they deem themselves "guilty" or "not guilty."

T.I.P. #65 Guided Imagery: The Courtroom Scene—Judge and Jury

T.I.P. #66 Guided Imagery: Your Board of Directors

T.I.P. #67 Guided Imagery: Forgiving the Dysfunctional Critics

T.I.P. #65 IMPLEMENTATION: Ask group participants to imagine they are in a courtroom and are under scrutiny from judge and jury. Who do the judge and jury represent from their own lives? Who do they remind them of? What would they be saying? Would there be anyone in the jury to support them? Who from their lives would the supporters be? Who would be their harshest critic? Ask group members to imagine one of their most stubborn self-judgments. Imagine what the judge would say. What would the jury say in their deliberations?

You also could have other group members be the jury. An individual group member could play the "jury" parts—either critic or supporter. Experiencing these messages acted out by judge and jury can be powerful.

T.I.P. #66 IMPLEMENTATION: Another variation is to have group members imagine they have a board of directors in their mind that orchestrates their attitudes and opinions. Who sits on their board of directors? Perhaps enlarge and photocopy for the group the shadow picture on the next page. Group members then can write in who people sitting on their "board" represent and what messages they are giving. In any given moment of difficulty, what do the board members say? What members of the board do they want to oust? What board members are more benevolent? What board members are undermining the "company stock?" What board members do they wish to retain? How would they change the makeup of the board? Are there vacancies on the board that need to be filled? They might find it helpful to close their eyes using guided imagery for completion of this activity.

TIP #67 IMPLEMENTATION: After identifying the critics, bosses, jury, and so forth, group participants can move on to imagining forgiveness of those toxic influences—forgiveness for being unhealthy and not knowing how to be healthier. Group members can be urged to relinquish the need to hold grudges, allowing compassion and forgiveness to replace resentments. In dealing with the most toxic influences, can members envision them in a court of law and the members themselves pardoning them and forgiving them by reason of insanity?

PROCESSING: These three activities can be powerful imagery techniques for looking at our inner "bosses" as well as for forgiving these critics and letting go of toxic influences. In facing one's inner critical messages as well as the benevolent supporters, one can be more in control of who is on the "company board" or on the "jury." Sometimes the old board or judge and jury need to be replaced. Sometimes a "re-trial" is warranted, or an overhaul of the entire board is in order!

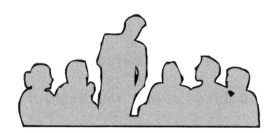

T.I.P. #68
EXERCISE: CRITIC AND CARETAKER

THEORY: Often we hold images in our minds of messages from our harshest critics more so than from our inner caregiver. All too often, my clients have kinder, caretaking thoughts for others and reserve the harshest, critical thoughts for themselves. This exercise helps group members confront and quell the critic and develop and bolster the caretaker role for themselves as they usually do for others.

IMPLEMENTATION: This is an "empty chair" exercise, similar to that found in Perls' Gestalt Therapy. Have two empty chairs next to the individual who is already seated, and instruct him/her to imagine one chair representing their Critic and the other representing their Caretaker. The person might have in mind a real-life dilemma. Ask the person to imagine that the Critic lets loose exactly what is in his/her mind. Following this, the client is asked to look at the Caretaker's chair and have this Caretaker defend and respond to the Critic. In a group situation, an alternative to the empty chair exercise is for the working group member to write out beforehand the Critic's remarks and have another group member role-play the Critic. Following the Critic scenario, the person also can supply lines for the Caretaker. Be sure to facilitate the group session ending on the Caretaker note rather than on the Critic note.

PROCESSING: This can be a very powerful exercise to encourage facing the inner critic, putting it in its place, and replacing negativity with more soothing self-statements from the caretaker within.

T.I.P. #69
ACTIVITY: WE ARE NOT ALONE

THEORY: A powerful insight we gain from group involvement is that we are not alone. Through the group experience, we recognize that there are common threads between ourselves and others. This exercise enlightens group members to the power of the sense of universality, encouraging group members to see themselves as part of a greater whole. It also encourages the ability to self-disclose in a non-threatening manner through this small group activity.

IMPLEMENTATION: Have group members break up into groups of four to five depending on the group size. Supply each group member with a piece of paper and pen and ask for one person to volunteer to be the secretary. Tell them they will have five to ten minutes to see how many things they can find in common among themselves. Encourage them to find at least ten. Once time is up, have each group share with the whole group the list they generated.

PROCESSING: This is a very fast-paced exercise that enables group members to find out about one another in a short period of time. It provides a relatively non-threatening way to get groups to self-disclose. After the groups share their findings, ask the whole group what impressions they have of the exercise in general. Did it cause them to feel more different or alike than others and why? Did they have more or less in common than they thought they would?

T.I.P.s #70 & #71
ACTIVITIES: WE ARE ALL NEWSWORTHY

THEORY: To promote self-discovery, in this activity self-disclosure, as well as disclosure to others, helps individuals crystallize what really is important to them, clarifies values, and helps identify positive aspects about themselves. Being in "the news" can help define core values and self-perceptions.

T.I.P. #70 EXTRA! EXTRA! READ ALL ABOUT IT!

T.I.P. #71 Activity: What's New?

T.I.P. #70 IMPLEMENTATION: Instruct the group: Create a front page of a newspaper about yourself. What would the headlines be? What would be of interest about you to let others know? Provide for the group the "headlines" format on the next page or ask that they create their own. Supply colored markers or pencils for a "colorful" look.

T.I.P. #71 IMPLEMENTATION: A great variation of this activity is for the entire group to create group headlines. They might feature the "top ten insights" achieved in group, as well as positive group learning experiences. There might be a sentence for each person in the group, announcing something about him/her or something he/she wants to share!

PROCESSING: This activity can at first be daunting but extremely powerful in both group and individual therapy. It encourages clients to believe they are important enough to be "newsworthy" and that their story is worth knowing.

★★★ *EXCLUSIVE!* ★★★

MY STORY

Volume 1, Issue 1   ★   ★   ★   Newsletter Date

A taste of what's inside:

My Hopes and Dreams........................... 2

Important People 3

What I've learned along
the way 4

What I am working on 5

Special Points of Interest About Me . . .

-
-
-
-
-

Highlights of "My Story"

_____

_____

_____

_____

_____

_____

_____

My Mission

_____

_____

_____

_____

_____

_____

T.I.P.s #72 & #73
DEMONSTRATION AND ACTIVITIES: MEASURING UP

THEORY: These are very powerful perspective-altering activities. Facing our mortality jolts us into the realization that we need to put things in perspective and make the most out of our limited time on earth. Facing our mortality, the fact we are going to die, can give us a new lease on life. These activities clearly are not recommended for clients who might be suicidal, but are appropriate and effective for healthier clients plagued with neurotic self-doubt and obsessive worrying.

T.I.P. #72 Life Lines: Putting It All in Perspective

T.I.P. #73 Parents Rule

T.I.P. #72 IMPLEMENTATION: Using a yardstick, with each inch representing 2 or 2 ½ years of life expectancy (being between 70 and 90), ask group participants questions such as the following: Where are you on this timeline? What have you done? What would you like to accomplish? What have you accomplished? Are some of the things that detract from your goals really important in the scheme of things? How long do you have with your spouse, children, work, etc? Have group participants find where they are on the yardstick. Ask the group: Faced with our mortality, are we going to give up some of our "woulda, coulda, shoulda" ways of thinking so we can free ourselves to make the most of our remaining time? Most are struck by this reality perspective, and some have found that this activity gives them a good life perspective. This activity also helps with goal setting and planning.

T.I.P. #73 IMPLEMENTATION: This yardstick visual is especially powerful for parents. So many times we struggle and take our children for granted, but it is a fact that we have them for a precious small amount of time. See where a child falls on the yardstick by age 18 (with each inch representing 2 or 2 ½ years). We see by this illustration that we have them for a very small portion of time, but the effects of how they are raised are longstanding. We need to be careful, as there can be long-lasting repercussions from our parental decisions and actions. This activity is great for parent education group members who need some inspiration to curb their anger and keep common childhood transgressions in perspective. (This perspective-gaining activity also might jolt some individuals to curb their drug or alcohol abuse.)

PROCESSING: The yardstick-inspired time perspective often jolts people into focusing on living in the present NOW! In the face of our finiteness, we can free ourselves of spending too much time going in random directions. This can be a reality check or a wake-up call, and likely will help group members become centered with a renewed focus of what is really important to them.

T.I.P. #74
SELF-ESTEEM DEMONSTRATION: HOW MUCH ARE YOU WORTH?

THEORY: This short visual demonstration allows individuals to see that no matter how crumbled and worn they feel, how tainted they feel they have become, whatever curve balls life has thrown at them up until now, they still have as much basic self-worth as anyone else. Poor self-esteem is at the root of many problems, and this short activity is aimed at strengthening poor self-esteem. This is a great exercise for people of all ages, children and adults.

IMPLEMENTATION: Take a 20-dollar bill (or even a 50-dollar bill for greater impact) and ask group participants to do anything they want to it as long as it remains intact as a 20-dollar bill. They can step on it, crumple it, flatten it out, or fold it one or more times. Pass the bill around the group and give a few people a chance to do something with it. Point out the idea that the bill is still worth the same thing— some bills might be worn and crumpled, some might be fresh and clean, but the worthiness is still the same. Emphasize that each of us is like that 20-dollar (or 50-dollar) bill. No matter what has happened to us in our lives, our actual self-worth remains intact even though we might feel crumpled, worn, and worthless.

PROCESSING: How often do people with low self-esteem feel they are not as worthy as others? This is a perfect exercise for showing participants that they are as worthy as anybody and for showing them that their value remains intact no matter how they feel about or see themselves in the grand scheme of things.

T.I.P. #75
DEMONSTRATION AND ACTIVITY: "COFFEE'S ON!"

THEORY: This hands-on activity is fun and takes very little time, but the lesson packs a punch! Who would think that a coffee filter could teach us about positive self-talk? This visual activity shows us that no matter how down we feel, things are looking up!

IMPLEMENTATION: Pass out to each participant a coffee filter with a flat bottom. Have group members break into pairs and ask one another what negative self-talk they carry, such as, "I should be more successful at this point in my life." The person doing the asking at the moment writes the negative self-talk his/her partner shared on the bottom of the filter and then writes a more positive message on the other side without showing the person. When both have written the more positive message for one another, they rise and drop their filters to the ground. The filter always turns itself right side up! At this moment, each partner is nicely surprised by the positive message the other has given to them. Note that if you sit down and try this, it might not right itself since you are not *giving it enough time.*

PROCESSING: I have used this activity with clients, in training groups, as well as in workplace-wellness groups. No matter what the forum, people enjoy this activity and find the analogy quite useful.

INSPIRATIONAL QUOTES

"We shall draw from the heart of suffering itself the means of inspiration and survival."

—Winston Churchill

* * *

"My imperfections and failures are as much a blessing from God as my successes and my talents, and I lay them both at His feet."

—Mahatma Gandhi

* * *

"Learn from yesterday, live for today, hope for tomorrow. The important thing is not to stop questioning."

—Albert Einstein

* * *

"People are just about as happy as they make up their minds to be."

—Abraham Lincoln

Inspirational Activities

T.I.P. #76
ANYWAY

THEORY: In her life work, as well as in the following passage, Mother Theresa has served as an inspiration for so many people from all walks of life. Her message offers a lifetime of love, compassion, forgiveness, and serenity to those who heed her advice to be filled with forgiveness and acceptance of life's unfairness. It is rumored that this passage was written on the walls of her orphanage in Calcutta, and appears to have been inspired by the Paradoxical Commandments, which were written by Kent M. Keith (who in 1968 wrote a similar message in a student handbook).

T.I.P. #76 Handout: "Anyway"

IMPLEMENTATION: You might have group participants take turns reading these lines, or you might choose to read the entire poem to them. Ask group members if they can relate to this poem—how their lives would be different if they incorporated the concepts of the poem. You might ask group members to add a line in the poem themselves that they would be willing to share in the group.

PROCESSING: This inspirational and thought-provoking passage can be the foundation for much productive discussion. Some relevant questions are: How can this passage help us make peace with others, as well as with our past? How can we let go of some of our preoccupations with comparing ourselves to others? What thought do we need to give up to live more in contentment and peace?

"ANYWAY"

Mother Theresa

People are often unreasonable, illogical, and self-centered;

   Forgive them anyway.

If you are kind, people may accuse you of selfish, ulterior motives;

   Be kind anyway.

If you are successful, you will win some false friends and some true enemies;

   Succeed anyway.

If you are honest and frank, people may cheat you;

   Be honest and frank anyway.

What you spend years building, someone could destroy overnight;

   Build anyway.

If you find serenity and happiness, they may be jealous;

   Be happy anyway.

The good you do today, people will often forget tomorrow;

   Do good anyway.

Give the world the best you have, and it may never be enough;

   Give the world the best you've got anyway.

You see, in the final analysis, it is between you and God;

   It was never between you and them anyway.

120

T.I.P. #77
FIVE STAGES OF GRIEVING

THEORY: The "five stages of grieving" by Elisabeth Kubler-Ross has long been the standard model for how people deal with loss. Even though originally these stages were conceptualized for facing the death of a loved one or facing one's own mortality, the model can be very powerful for understanding the loss of a relationship, marriage, job, dream, or even just the illusion that you thought a person was someone he/she isn't. I use this handout often when dealing with clients who are depressed and/or suffering from the demise of a relationship, including marital breakup.

T.I.P. #77 Handout: Five Stages of Grieving

IMPLEMENTATION: This sheet has proved helpful for those struggling with many types of loss. Have a client identify what stages he/she has gone through and where he/she is stuck in grieving the loss. The loss can be a psychological loss as well as a "real-life" loss—such as the facing of one's aging and mortality. It might be breaking through denial and facing the reality that your spouse is not who you "hoped" he/she would be. Those going through a painful separation or divorce find this model extremely helpful in learning to grow into acceptance.

PROCESSING: It is unavoidable—we all go through stages of grieving when overcoming hurt and loss. That is a necessary part of life, as Judith Viorst explains in her book *Necessary Losses*. Only by leaving and being left, letting go and moving on, can we grow from inevitable loss and replace the loss with personal growth. If we do not choose growth, we will be immobilized from the loss and become "stuck." How painful it has been for so many people who have carried to their graves the incomplete mourning of losses in their lives, those who have never grown through to the final stage of acceptance.

FIVE STAGES OF GRIEVING

(based on the teachings of Elisabeth Kubler-Ross)

Five Stages	Of Death and Dying	Of Healing a Memory
DENIAL	I avoid facing the likelihood of my death. I cannot face mortality. I feel and act as though I am invincible.	I don't admit I either am or ever was hurt. I don't face the reality of my unrealized dreams and illusions. I see things like I want to see them, and not as they are.
ANGER	I blame others for letting death hurt and destroy me. I am filled with resentment and can't forgive.	I blame others for hurting and destroying me. Others are responsible for my pain, and I can't forgive. Anger and "shoulds" consume me.
BARGAINING	I set up conditions to be fulfilled before I'm ready to die. If I do, then I can avoid reality and make things as I want them to be.	I set up conditions to be fulfilled before I'm ready to forgive others and myself. If I act in a certain way, perhaps I can get others to change their minds or behaviors.
DEPRESSION	I blame myself for letting death take over. I failed in my life—I didn't accomplish what I had hoped—I have much regret.	I blame myself for letting hurt destroy me. I failed and am powerless, ashamed, and helpless. Hopelessness, regret, and despair consume me.
ACCEPTANCE	I'm ready to die. I've made peace with others and myself. I have come to terms with my mortality.	I look forward to growth from hurt and change. I can accept and forgive myself and others. I can let go of impossible dreams, illusions, "shoulds," and expectations without a veil of delusion.

Judith A. Belmont, M.S. *(2006)* • *The Therapeutic Toolbox: 103 Group Activities and T.I.P.S.* • www.worksiteinsights.com • All rights reserved.

T.I.P.s #78–81
QUOTE THERAPY

THEORY: Quotes from famous and respected people from the past can be powerful. Quotes can provide comfort and insight, help develop optimism, and promote hope. Use these quotes for inspiration and as springboards for discussion, all the while planting the idea that there is hope!

T.I.P. #78 Give Me a Sign!

T.I.P. #79 Quotes for Therapeutic Group Work

T.I.P. #79 Handout: Quotes for Therapeutic Group Work

T.I.P. #80 Confucius for a Day

T.I.P. #81 Words of Wisdom I've Learned . . .

T.I.P. #78 IMPLEMENTATION: Use quotes in your waiting room or common area, outside your door, in a Plexiglas holder, changing them frequently depending on the amount of traffic in the area. This sets a great mood for those coming in and out of your door. Staff and clients alike will likely make special trips by your door to see the quote of the week! Caution: I assure you that you will need to change out quotes from time to time or else have to hear about it from co-workers looking forward to the next and the next!

T.I.P. #79 IMPLEMENTATION: The "Quotes for Therapeutic Group Work" handout contains quotes chosen for individual and group therapy; of course, you can choose quotes that pertain to any specific topic of group focus. Quotes are not only inspirational, they are excellent springboards for discussion. Quotes on just about anything can be found on the internet. Here are a few of the many sites: http://www.quotationspage.com/, http://www.inspirational-quotes.info/, and http://www.brainyquote.com/.

T.I.P. #80 IMPLEMENTATION: Have group members be "Confucius for a Day"—we all have our own pearls of wisdom! Give participants about 15 minutes to make up one quote each of their own each. Have them explain to the group what each quote means. An interesting variation could be to put the quotes in a hat and then as you pull them out and read them, group members can try to guess each author.

T.I.P. #81 IMPLEMENTATION: Another activity variation for using quotes is to have group participants finish this statement: "In my life, one important lesson I have learned is . . ." You then might read a few samples from the book, *Live and Learn and Pass It On,* by H. Jackson Brown.

PROCESSING: The goal of these quote-centered activities is to encourage group participants to uncover their own inner wisdom. These quotes can be used as inspirations. Even though they are often short and sweet, the impact can pack a wallop! Just as phrases from the Bible can be a source of comfort for some, so can quotes of respected figures in history pack a lot of meaning in one phrase!

QUOTES FOR THERAPEUTIC GROUP WORK

"Nothing is good or bad but thinking makes it so."

—Shakespeare (Hamlet)

* * *

"People are disturbed not by things but the views they take of them."

—Epictetus (1st century AD)

* * *

"No one can hurt your feelings without your permission."

—Eleanor Roosevelt

* * *

"If you are distressed by anything external, the pain is not due to the thing itself, but to your estimate of it; and this you have the power to revoke at any moment."

—Marcus Aurelius

* * *

"I don't like that man. I must get to know him better."

—Abraham Lincoln

* * *

"No one can make you feel inferior without your consent."

—Eleanor Roosevelt

* * *

"A smile is a curve that sets everything straight."

—Phyllis Diller

125

"All that we are is the result of what we have thought."

—Buddha (563 BC–483 BC)

* * *

"Anyone can become angry. That is easy. But to be angry with the right person, to the right degree, at the right time, for the right purpose and in the right way—that is not easy."

—Aristotle (384 BC–322 BC)

* * *

"Forgiveness is giving up the possibility of a better past."

—Mahatma Gandhi

* * *

"The weak can never forgive. Forgiveness is the attribute of the strong."

—Mahatma Ghandhi

* * *

"Forgiveness is the fragrance that the violet sheds on the heel that has crushed it."

—Mark Twain

* * *

"Holding on to anger is like holding on to a hot coal with the intent of throwing it at someone else; you are the one who gets burned."

—Buddha

T.I.P.s #82–#84
THE POWER OF SONG

THEORY: Songs have the potential to cut right to the core. Songs are often central in our client's lives, and too often neglected in therapy. Both in individual and group therapy songs can become tools for self exploration and strength. Often the power of song is untapped in terms of its potential.

T.I.P. #82 Soul Tunes

T.I.P. #83 Make Your Own Lyrics

T.I.P. #84 Change Those Dysfunctional Lyrics!

T.I.P. #82 IMPLEMENTATION: Bring in a song to play that demonstrates a concept you want to discuss in group that day. You may have group members close their eyes to experience better the meaning of the message. Have the group describe how they felt listening to the song. Popular and self-affirming songs that may be excellent choices for therapeutic groups include: "I Hope You Dance," by Leeann Womack, "Hero," by Mariah Carey; and "The Greatest Love of All," by Whitney Houston. Alternatives to these popular songs are songs from Jana Stanfield (http://www.janastanfield.com/), whose CDs are full of songs reflecting therapeutic messages. Albert Ellis, Father of Rational Emotive Behavior Therapy, has a CD called "A Garland of Rational Songs" (http://www.rebt.org/), which are humorous songs sung by Albert Ellis himself to promote concepts of cognitive therapy. I often use these in presenting to groups, and they are very humorous, entertaining, and powerful. You also can request that participants bring songs to group that they would like to share to express something about themselves.

T.I.P. #83 IMPLEMENTATION: A variation on T.I.P. #82 is to choose a song that everyone knows and have the group make their own words based on the self-help principles the group wants to include. Have the group brainstorm on what therapeutic messages they want to include, such as "forgive yourself" or "forgive others," and transform these ideas into lyrics to reflect these messages.

T.I.P. #84 IMPLEMENTATION: When we think of the "whiny women victim songs" of the 60s and 70s and many other songs throughout our lifetimes (e.g., "I love him, I love him, and where he goes I'll follow!"), we can recognize codependent themes in many of them. Maybe our new revised rational lyrics would not make a gold record, but we can undo some of the effects of the dysfunctional messages that

127

bombard us in popular culture. Have group members brainstorm on songs with dysfunctional messages and rewrite the titles into more rational alternatives. Here are some examples:

Song	***More Rational Message***
"I Can't Stop Loving You"—Ray Charles	"It's Hard to Stop Loving You"
"You Make Me Feel Like a Natural Woman —Aretha Franklin (Note: The downside is, you can make me feel artificial!)	"I Feel 'Real' When I Am with You"
"There Goes My Reason for Living, There Goes My Everything"—Englebert Humperdinck	"There Goes Someone I Care a Lot About, but I Am Not Worthless Without Her!"
"You Make Me So Very Happy!" —Blood, Sweat and Tears	"I Am Happy When I Am with You!"

PROCESSING: Sometimes songs can touch us in ways that spoken words cannot. These activities offer possibilities for interaction and lightheartedness in dealing with serious messages. The power of song should not be underestimated. This tool can unleash feelings and can provide guidance for positive self-affirmation. Rewriting lyrics or titles can be music to group members' ears!

T.I.P. #85
POWER OF CINEMATHERAPY

THEORY: Cinematherapy has provided me with powerful tools for working both with individuals and groups. Relating to characters in movies can be powerful aids to understanding oneself.

IMPLEMENTATION: In individual therapy, I might suggest a movie that relates to the individual, and ask him/her to rent and watch it, and then we can discuss it. In a group situation, including workplace wellness groups or mental health in-service training groups, I provide video clips to show important therapeutic principles. Another option would be to show an entire movie and discuss it over a few weeks' time, depending on the timing of the group. There are many ways to use movies. My favorite movie depicting psychological issues is *Ordinary People.* In this movie, one can recognize themes relating to personality disorders, depression, suicidal behavior, unhealthy coping skills, co-dependency, forgiveness, communication, hope, and healing—all in one powerful movie! Here are a few books that you can use as resources to find movies that fit in with your treatment goal:

> *Reel People: Finding Ourselves in the Movies*—Gluss
>
> *Rent Two Films and Let's Talk in the Morning*—Hesley
>
> *Reel Psychiatry: Movie Portrayals of Psychiatric Conditions*—Robinson
>
> *Movies & Mental Illness*—Wedding

PROCESSING: Cinematherapy has an advantage over more traditional therapy in that one can experience and visualize concepts through memorable media. The power of movies is unlimited in its potential.

QUOTES ON MINDFULNESS

"Do not dwell in the past, do not dream of the future, concentrate the mind on the present moment."

—Buddha

* * *

"You must live in the present, launch yourself on every wave, find your eternity in each moment."

—Henry David Thoreau

* * *

"If we open a quarrel between the past and the present, we shall find that we have lost the future."

—Winston Churchill

* * *

"The secret of health for both mind and body is not to mourn for the past, worry about the future, or anticipate troubles, but to live in the present moment wisely and earnestly."

—Buddha

Imagery and Mindfulness

T.I.P. #86
PUTTING THE COLOR BACK INTO YOUR WORLD!

THEORY: In our busy lives, we often are oblivious to our surroundings. As we focus on selected thoughts and feelings, we tend to shut out much of our environment. Especially during mental distress, we often block out the stimuli and beauty around us, selecting to focus on thoughts and feelings relating to the disturbance. This exercise helps groups work on developing the ability to be "mindful," which increases the ability to achieve emotional and mental balance.

IMPLEMENTATION: Request that group participants look briefly around them, and then ask them to close their eyes. With their eyes closed, ask them to recount all the things around them that they remember with the color red, color blue, color black, and so on. Then allow the group to open their eyes and look again at the colors around them. Then, ask them to close their eyes again and answer the same questions. This time, their answers likely will be much more directed and detailed.

PROCESSING: Relevant questions are as follows: "What did you learn from this exercise?" "How can this lesson be applied to your awareness in everyday life?" "How can mindfulness and awareness aid in limiting obsessive thinking and unhealthy perseverating?" "What are we missing in our daily lives due to our lack of mindfulness?" Mindfulness is a vital strategy of Dialectical Behavioral Therapy (DBT) and can be applied easily to treatment resistant and high risk clients, such as those with Borderline Personality Disorder.

T.I.P. #87
ARE YOU A HUMAN DOING OR A HUMAN BEING?

THEORY: Mindfulness is an important component of DBT, and meditative exercises are a vital component of DBT for high risk clients. This mindfulness exercise helps people understand how to move from being mostly a "human doing" to a "human being" who more fully experiences the present moment.

IMPLEMENTATION: Ask group participants to focus for five to ten minutes on the one thing they can count on for the rest of their lives—their breath. As they focus on breathing, ask them to keep their eyes open and focus on their senses rather than their thoughts. What are they seeing? Look at only one thing at a time. If they are "thinking about" and interpreting what they are seeing, that is no longer being "mindful." Urge them to attempt to perceive without input from judgments, interpretations, and evaluations (such as, "I like the color," or "I think this looks out of place"). If they find themselves having a running commentary of what they are experiencing, they should try not to judge that but to gently refocus themselves on the present moment and the sensations being experienced now.

PROCESSING: This exercise helps participants become alert to and aware of their surroundings, and emphasizes that "thinking about thinking" is not being mindful. Being mindful suspends judgment and evaluation—things are accepted as they are. By not analyzing and interpreting, individuals can quell the inner noise and fully experience the present, while letting go of distracting thoughts and judgments.

T.I.P.s #88 & #89
DESCRIBING AND OBSERVING

THEORY: Marsha Linehan, in her DBT work on mindfulness, explains that observing and describing are important elements of mindfulness. These two short activities show how these concepts imply sensing without judgment and evaluation to allow people to experience the "here and now."

T.I.P. #88 Mindfulness Activity: Describing

T.I.P. #89 Mindfulness Activity: Observing

T.I.P. #88 IMPLEMENTATION: In Linehan's exercise in her VHS tape, "This One Moment," she makes an angry appearing face and questions what observers are seeing. Most people would say they see an angry face, which implies interpretation and not mindfulness. A mindful description would be "facial grimacing," "twisted mouth," "furrowed eyebrows," and so forth. Linehan cautions against treating interpretations as facts.

T.I.P. #89 IMPLEMENTATION: In this exercise, also from the same Linehan VHS tape, she asks participants to put one hand on a table and observe what they are seeing. If one starts to have a running commentary focusing on coolness, feeling the table is hard, and so on, then one is shifting from mindfulness to evaluation. Observing without interpretation—quelling the inner dialog—is the goal of this exercise.

PROCESSING: These are very simple exercises demonstrating the difference between describing and observing from inferring and judging. Mindfulness is something that does not necessarily come naturally, and is to be practiced and reinforced. Underlying DBT is the assumption that too much interpretation and subjectivity limits our ability to be "mindful," which in turn renders us unable to cope effectively under stress.

T.I.P. #90
ACTIVITY: NOURISHING YOURSELF MINDFULLY

THEORY: So often we eat only to realize that the food on our plate is gone and we don't remember eating it all! We often eat on the run, eat too fast, and all but inhale our food. Because eating is so much a part of our daily activities, the act of eating mindfully is a great way to teach and practice the art of mindfulness.

IMPLEMENTATION: Prepare a small sealed package containing a small piece of food such as crackers or raisins; open it and offer it to group members. Introduce the concept of mindfulness, explaining how eating mindfully can help group members practice mindfulness frequently and successfully in their everyday lives. As they take a bite, ask them to eat as slowly as possible, for a matter of minutes and not seconds. Have them close their eyes and guide them visually in an experience where they imagine where the food came from, imagining the ingredients of the food, the origins of these foods, and absorb what has transpired to get that piece of food to be experienced presently. For example, in the case of a cracker, imagine the wheat in the fields, the sun beating on the grains, perhaps feeling the sensation of warmth within. Imagine the mines where the salt came from, the water, and the processing and logistics it took to bring this food to us presently. Sample questions include: "What did you learn from this exercise?" "How can this lesson be applied to your awareness in everyday life?" "How can mindfulness and awareness aid in limiting obsessive thinking and unhealthy perseverating?" "What are we missing in our daily lives due to our lack of mindfulness?"

PROCESSING: This is yet another activity to apply mindfulness in everyday life. Mindfulness is a vital strategy of DBT and can be applied easily to treatment resistant and high risk clients, such as those with Borderline Personality Disorder.

T.I.P. #91
ACTIVITY: IMAGERY MIND STRETCHER I

THEORY: This activity helps people alter their perceptions with a bit of "mind stretching." This fun group activity encourages "out of the box" thinking. This is particularly helpful with clients who have difficulty verbalizing their feelings about themselves. It is an interesting activity to do within the group context, which leads to camaraderie, insights into self and others, and just plain fun!

IMPLEMENTATION: Write the following questions on a flipchart or board and give group participants five to ten minutes to write their responses:

If you were something that sparkles, what would it be and why?

If you were an animal, what would it be and why?

If you were a metal object, what would it be and why?

If you were a food, what would it be and why?

Looking around, what in the room best describes you?

If you were a piece of nature other than yourself, what would it be and why?

Members take turns sharing and explaining their answers.

PROCESSING: This activity can lead to very interesting discussions and revelations. After everyone has a turn to share his/her answers, allow some time for questions about the answers and further explanations. This is an excellent sharing activity that provides a chance to look at ourselves in a different way and encourages creative thinking.

T.I.P. #92
ACTIVITY: IMAGERY MIND STRETCHER II

THEORY: This exercise is ideal following T.I.P. #91, Imagery Mind Stretcher I. Since most often those in treatment have a hard time dealing with at least one other person in their lives, have them answer the following questions for one person of their choice who poses difficulty in their own lives. This will help group members put these individuals in perspective through the activity of "mind stretching." It is an interesting activity to do within the group context, which leads to camaraderie, insights into self and others, and lots of fun.

IMPLEMENTATION: Write the following questions on a flipchart or board and give group participants five to ten minutes to write their responses concerning an individual who poses difficulty for them. Ask them to be prepared to explain each answer.

If this person were something that sparkles, what would it be and why?

If this person were an animal, what would it be and why?

If this person were a metal object, what would it be and why?

If this person were a food, what would it be and why?

Looking around, what in the room best describes this person?

If this person were a piece of nature, what would it be and why?

Have members, one at a time, introduce their relationship to the person they have picked and briefly explain their answers.

PROCESSING: Compare and contrast the answers they gave for themselves in T.I.P. #91 and for the other person in T.I.P. #92. You might use similar processing questions as those shown in Mind Stretcher I. This activity can lead to insight and increased perspective of the other person.

T.I.P. #93
ACTIVITY: BODY IMAGE IMAGERY

THEORY: This very powerful exercise was developed by Eileen Belmont Margolis, educational specialist at the Renfrew House in Philadelphia. Renfrew is an inpatient facility for treatment of those with eating disorders. Margolis has used this activity successfully with clients; it is designed to increase awareness that despite obsession with outward appearance, it is what is on the inside that is most important.

IMPLEMENTATION: Clients are asked to close their eyes and imagine a person they admire very much. What makes this person special? How do you feel with that person? With that person in mind, in a few words or sentences, describe him/her and write it down. Share with the group not necessarily who that person is but the written description. Invariably, shared descriptions have very little or nothing to do with the outside of a person. Instead of focusing on thinness, clients tend to write down characteristics that people possess on the inside. Contrast that with the way clients view and judge themselves, with so much emphasis on "thinness" and general outside appearance.

PROCESSING: Despite the fact that those with eating disorders such as Anorexia are obsessive about outside appearances, what they most often value in others is inner beauty. This is a great activity for those who have different standards for themselves than for others. In order to see their own inner beauty, perhaps they can give themselves the same courtesy they give to others and look beneath the surface at the inner person.

T.I.P. #94
PROGRESSIVE RELAXATION

THEORY: Progressive relaxation is a great way to help people learn to relax. All too often we are all tensed up and do not realize the extent of that tension.

IMPLEMENTATION: While playing relaxing background music (I enjoy "Timeless Motion," a CD that includes Pachelbel's *Canon in D*), have clients close their eyes. Beginning with the feet, have participants tense up parts of their bodies, have them hold it a moment, tense up a bit more, and then relax while feeling the contrast between the tension felt just a moment ago and now. Systematically go through parts of the body, tensing the legs, buttocks, clenching the arms, hands, neck, face, and so on.

PROCESSING: After the exercise, you might bring group participants on a guided imagery such as in T.I.P. #95, or have them open their eyes and express how they feel now versus before the exercise. Did they find the progressive tensing and releasing helpful for relaxation, or did they find it more stressful?

T.I.P. #95
GUIDED IMAGERY

THEORY: After experiencing progressive relaxation in T.I.P. #94, clients find that guided imagery also helps them learn to relax and slow down.

IMPLEMENTATION: A worthwhile reference for learning the basics of guided imagery is *Guided Imagery for Groups* by Andrew E. Schwartz, 1995, Duluth, MN: Whole Person Associates. When constructing a guided imagery experience, consider the following images as suggestions:

- Smile, Sparkle, Alert, Amused Mind, Calm Body

- A Jewel Box—Describe the jewels; what do they represent?

- You are on an island, or somewhere in nature; what does it look like? How does it feel?

- Imagine you are by a river. Clasp your hands with messages you want to let go of; surrender the messages to the water and watch them drift.

- Imagine you are in a classroom and the board is filled with learning. What does it say? Then go up to the chalkboard. What will you write? What lesson will you teach?

PROCESSING: Clients might feel energized and refreshed as they symbolically address issues while learning techniques to relax.

QUOTES ON SAYING GOODBYE

"Every goodbye is the birth of a memory."

—Dutch Proverb

* * *

"A memory lasts forever. Never does it die. True friends stay together and never say 'goodbye'."

—Unknown

* * *

"Goodbyes are sad, yet they should also be cherished because it is this word that causes all memories to come flooding back as if they had happened yesterday."

—Unknown

* * *

"A moment lasts all of a second, but the memory lives on forever."

—Unknown

Group Closings

T.I.P. #96
VISUAL REMINDER: CRISIS PAVES THE WAY FOR GROWTH AND CHANGE

THEORY: I often close a group or workshop by keeping on a positive note and reminding participants that crises and difficulty pave the way for growth and change. The bad times don't have to last forever! (This visual demonstration is also a helpful concept for stress management workshops.)

IMPLEMENTATION: President Kennedy is noted for mentioning in one of his speeches that the Chinese symbol for "crisis" is made up of the two symbols standing for "danger" plus "opportunity." Show participants this symbol or provide a photocopy of it for them to serve as an inspirational reminder that in the midst of upheaval, opportunity presents itself for growth and healing.

PROCESSING: This symbol underscores the notion that behind adversity is potential for growth.

The Chinese Symbol for Crisis

Danger   Opportunity

T.I.P. #97
ACTIVITY: THE WEB WE CREATE

THEORY: In a group experience, we weave connections between each other. The sign of a successful group experience is to feel a part of something larger than oneself—that you are not alone, isolated, and alienated. Hopefully, in a group one can feel free to express oneself, listen to others, and become stronger. As Gestalt therapy exhorts, "the whole is greater than the sum of its parts!"

IMPLEMENTATION: With a ball of yarn, begin by addressing another group member by asking a question or saying something positive—whichever process you choose. This is done while tossing the ball of yarn to that person while you hold the other end. This person in turn holds onto the yarn while tossing the rest of the ball to someone else, asking a question or expressing something positive about that next person, and so on until all group members are holding yarn. Depending on the size of the group, how many times the yarn goes around, group members may take turns trying to sit on the web! As the song goes, "He's not heavy, he's my brother!"

PROCESSING: This is an excellent demonstration of the interconnectedness of us all. Figuratively, we are part of a web, where the "We" in web overcomes the "I" of isolation. Discuss how the web we create makes us enriched and interconnected in a greater sense of "wholeness." The main idea that often emerges is the sense of universality—that one is not alone. Quite the contrary, other people have similar issues and struggles, and knowing this can serve as a source of comfort.

T.I.P. #98
ACTIVITY: THE "GEM" INSIDE OF ME

THEORY: When a group ends, this offers an ideal opportunity to create a time and space to express positive feedback to each group member. Rather than leaving a group "hanging," this closure exercise works on two levels: it gives the group a sense of overall group closure, and it gives individuals a sense of personal closure from the group experience. People leave the group with a renewed sense of themselves as they receive positive feedback from each group member, along with a group memento.

IMPLEMENTATION: My favorite closing ritual is to use rock gems—the little polished stones that you can buy inexpensively at novelty stores. They are multicolored and have various shapes. I suggest to the group that the stones symbolize the gem inside of us. Each member gets to pick a colorful gem to use for this activity. With one person in focus at a time, the gem is passed around to each group member, and each says something positive about the person from experience in group with him/her. When the gem is passed back to the individual in focus, that person also says something positive about himself/herself or something special he/she learned in the group experience. Each member gets to keep this symbolic memento from the group experience, reminding him/her of the positive messages about the "gems" inside of us.

PROCESSING: After all members take turns and the gems are back to their group members, ask the group how they feel about hearing positive things about themselves. Many people have a hard time with compliments, and this can stimulate a lot of discussion. The discussion might lead to how it feels to end the group. Point out that the gems can remind them of what they learned in this experience and what they discovered about the "gems" inside themselves and others.

T.I.P. #99
ACTIVITY: TOUCHING BASE

THEORY: The closing of any group session can benefit from "touching base" and leaving participants on a positive and thoughtful note. This activity helps bring some closure to the group and also gives the facilitator feedback about what made an impression on the participants for use in future planning.

IMPLEMENTATION: There's nothing fancy about this concept, but it works for any group, whether it be a therapeutic group, training seminar, or workplace wellness group. I ask all participants to go around and share one thing they gained or learned in the current session. It is always very interesting to hear participants' answers and reinforces what works. Participants also leave on a positive note. I generally do not use the closings to ask for constructive feedback on what they did not like; I ask for those impressions after a certain activity if appropriate but not at the group closing where the goal is to end positively.

PROCESSING: This is a quick and simple exercise that gives everyone a chance to express themselves and summarize their experience with the group. This exercise promotes a sense of commonality and universality because often many participants share similar feelings and reactions, and these comments reinforce the personal reactions from the shared experiences.

T.I.P. #100
HEAD, HEART, AND HAND

THEORY: In experiential groups, learning is ideally accomplished on three dimensions—thought, feeling, and behavior. In experiential groups, learning will be not only cerebral but incorporated into a feelings level, and the insight into thought and feelings hopefully will spur new behaviors in real life outside of group. This activity gets participants in tune with these three concepts of learning and helps them identify the three different modalities of insight they have achieved.

T.I.P. #100 Handout: Head, Heart, Hand

IMPLEMENTATION: Use this sheet or just have the group participants visualize what they have learned, either in a given session or throughout the entire group duration if the group is terminating. This helps them to differentiate thoughts, feelings and behaviors. This also helps each individual review the progress he/she has made and some specific concepts learned. Have participants share what they envisioned or wrote.

PROCESSING: This is a very positive way to end a group, as participants are given a chance to reflect and share their responses and hear the responses of others.

HEAD, HEART, HAND

What I have learned:

HEAD (i.e., on a thought level)

HEART (i.e., on a feeling level)

HAND (i.e., on a behavioral level, either within the group or to do in the future)

T.I.P.s #101 & #102
MEMOS TO MYSELF AND OTHERS

THEORY: The end of a group experience is an ideal time to reflect on what one has learned. Although the "Touching Base" exercise in T.I.P. #99 provides the opportunity for all participants to share what they have learned or gained from the group, some learning might be of a more personal nature or an individual might not want to share some very personal impressions out loud. This activity provides opportunity for self-reflection and self-expression.

T.I.P. #101 Activity: Letter—To Yours Truly from Yours Truly

T.I.P. #102 Activity: Letter—You Made an Impression on Me . . .

T.I.P. #101 IMPLEMENTATION: All participants are given some stationery and a pen and are asked to write a letter to themselves. Instruct them to share what they have learned or gained from the group experience, and inform them that this letter will be sent to them in two or three months. Have them address an envelope, put the letter in it, and seal it when they are finished. Allow about 20 minutes for this activity.

T.I.P. #102 IMPLEMENTATION: Another writing activity that allows for some privacy as it does not call for thoughts to be shared out loud is as follows: Dole out to each group member a stack of three by five index cards, each with a different group member's name written at the top. Have group members take about 20 minutes or so to write in one or two sentences something they learned from or liked about each of the other group members, signing their name at the bottom of each card. You could include all the cards for each group member in the same envelope as the "Yours Truly" letter, or you might collect and disperse each individual's cards to be taken home that very day. These cards often will be cherished by group members, who can refer to the cards any time they want to be reminded that others thought of something special about them.

PROCESSING: These activities are great ways to provide ongoing reminders for individuals leaving the therapeutic group experience. In a few months, how quickly one can forget important lessons, and the note cards and letter can provide opportunity to be reminded of healthy messages from the group experience. One might see this as a type of time capsule that gives individuals tangible evidence of a slice of their lives in crucial times when they're needing a reminder of a more positive time. The feedback to them might be a source of strength, inspiration, and faith in their ability to connect with others, especially in tough times!

T.I.P. #103
THE THERAPIST'S TOOLBOX

THEORY: Now, it's your turn! Usually at the end of a group experience, I ask group participants what they have learned. Likewise, now that we are at the end of this book, it's your turn to review what you learned here. What tools have you gained?

IMPLEMENTATION: Consider the major tools and T.I.P.S you learned throughout this workbook, and either write in or just imagine yourself writing in the tools below the T.I.P.S. you found most helpful. Have you thought of how you can incorporate some of the ideas to fit your work? My hope in writing this book is to share some very special techniques that I have found effective and hope you will be able to find them helpful also!

PROCESSING: This is just a start—hopefully you will be inspired to collect your own activities, handouts, and ideas, and this workbook will spur you to use a myriad of techniques and activities in your therapeutic work.

AFTERWORD

Hopefully there have been some T.I.P.S. that you already have begun to use with clients. I know that many of you reading this workbook have also used your own ideas and tools that have been successful in treatment of either individuals or groups. I invite you to share them in my future book that will be a therapeutic collaborative workbook. If you would be interested in sharing your ideas, please submit them to JABelmont@worksiteinsights.com.

All references will be cited and credit given within the workbook. For more information, please contact me for submission requirements.

Judith Belmont, M.S.